TEXAS DIVORCE GUIDE

Everything You Need to Know About Divorce in Texas

HARRY L. MUNSINGER, J.D., PH.D.

Archway Publishing books may be ordered through booksellers or by contacting:

Archway Publishing
1663 Liberty Drive
Bloomington, IN 47403
www.archwaypublishing.com
1 (888) 242-5904

ISBN: 978-1-4808-5379-9 (sc)
ISBN: 978-1-4808-5378-2 (e)

Library of Congress Control Number: 2017916337

Print information available on the last page.

Archway Publishing rev. date: 10/27/2017

My book is dedicated to all those considering a divorce.

Contents

Preface

The purpose of this book is to explain what happens during a Texas divorce and help you get through it with minimal stress. The first set of chapters will help you decide if your marriage is over and whether you need a divorce and discusses the causes of divorce. Section two prepares you for divorce, alerts you to the major difficulties you will face during a divorce, helps you be realistic about the potential outcomes, and explains how to cope with grief. Chapters in section three show you how to decide if a collaborative divorce or litigation is right for you, teaches you how to tell the kids about your divorce and how to find the right divorce attorney, and debunks major divorce myths. Section four deals with divorce fears, suggests how to handle a narcissistic spouse during divorce, advises you about how to survive a divorce financially, and trains you to negotiate and compromise. The fifth set of chapters explains Texas law on child custody, spousal support, child support, and how to divide assets. The final set of chapters advises you about dating during divorce, explains the purpose of mediation, suggests ways to make the holidays fun during a divorce, and reminds you to revise your estate plan after the divorce is final.

Ways to Use My Book

There are at least three ways you can use this book. One is to read chapters as they become relevant to your divorce. This is the most efficient way to use my book, but you won't have as clear an understanding of the entire process until you finish. A second approach is to read the entire book from start to finish. This approach will give you a good understanding of what you will face during a Texas divorce and may help relieve your anxiety about the process. Reading the entire book before you begin your divorce takes more time but gives you lots of useful information. My personal recommendation is that you read the first seventeen chapters of the book and then find a divorce attorney you like based on the recommendations of chapter 17. After that, you may read all the remaining chapters or review them as they become relevant. By following this approach, you can decide if you need a divorce, gain an understanding of how divorce works in Texas, choose between a collaborative or litigated divorce, and learn how to find the right divorce lawyer. Once you find the right attorney, share the book with him or her and then read all the remaining chapters or review the sections relevant to your divorce as you work with your lawyer.

A Divorce Need Not Be Stressful

Getting a divorce can be a difficult and confusing experience, especially if you choose to litigate the dispute. If you read my book and follow the guidance of a collaborative divorce attorney, you can avoid most of the stress, clear up the confusion, and navigate the pitfalls of a divorce without losing your mind, your money, or your children. *Texas Divorce Guide* will tell you everything you need to know about getting through a Texas divorce without going crazy. If you have questions or comments, please contact me at harry@harrymunsinger.com.

Ten Signs You Need a Divorce

A Summary of Factors in Your Relationship That Indicate You Probably Need a Divorce

"There has to be a divorce and stuff, Irene — you can't just *resign!*"

Considering a divorce? Not sure what to do? Being uncertain about whether to divorce or work on your marriage is normal because there's no way to be sure you're doing the right thing. Being unhappy is stressful, and we generally want to end the pain by doing something. However, don't rush into divorce simply to avoid pain and uncertainty. Take your time ending a marriage. It's a big decision, so before deciding to divorce, consider the following signs you might want to untie the knot.

You Have a Sexless Marriage.

I don't mean you haven't had sex for a week or so. I'm talking about no sex for six months or longer. If you aren't having sex, why are you staying together? If sex has become a power struggle or a source of rejection, your marriage may be over, and you may need a divorce.

You Can't Compromise.

All couples argue. However, if you and your spouse have the same fight over and over without settling anything, your marriage is in trouble. There has to be give and take to make a marriage work. If you don't know how to compromise, your marriage isn't working, and you may need to get out or learn to meet each other somewhere in the middle to resolve disagreements.

One of You Is Cheating.

Most people think cheating on your spouse means having sex with someone else, but that's not the only way to be unfaithful. If you are cheating on your spouse emotionally by paying attention to someone else or cheating financially by hiding money or spending extravagantly, it's time to give your spouse some respect. Either stop cheating or get a divorce.

You Show Contempt for Each Other.

Arguments and anger are inevitable in a marriage. It's how you handle disagreements that makes the difference between a healthy marriage and a dysfunctional relationship. If your disputes disintegrate into shouting matches where you call each other awful names, leave angry, and give each other the cold shoulder for a week, that's a sign you should learn to forgive and forget, or consider a divorce.

Marital Counseling Isn't Working.

Marriage counseling requires a commitment by both spouses to work on the relationship and make changes in their behavior. If one spouse is trying to fix the marriage while the other isn't, you're wasting your time and money going to marital counseling. You both need to make a commitment to fix the marriage, or you need to get out of the relationship.

The Relationship Is Abusive.

If you live in a home with shoving, hitting, or threats of violence, you should leave immediately. There is no excuse for physical abuse. The cycle of family violence begins with a single shove, followed by remorse. If you let it go, you risk falling into a recurring cycle of violence, remorse, blame, and more violence. When physical abuse happens, get out immediately.

You Don't Trust Each Other.

A healthy marriage requires love, trust, and respect. If you and your spouse don't trust each other, it may be time to rebuild trust or get out of the marriage.

Your Interactions Are Mostly Negative.

All couples have problems. Experts say the ratio of positive to negative interactions in a healthy marriage should be about five to one. If your interactions are mostly negative, it's time to consider a divorce or a serious change in the way you interact.

You Can't Communicate Feelings.

Are you afraid to share feelings with your spouse because that might cause a fight? Does your spouse ignore or reject you when you tell him or her how you feel? Does your spouse seem not to listen, or is he or she too defensive? Are your needs being met in the marriage? If you can't share feelings with each other, it may be time to divorce.

You Put Each Other Last.

If your spouse is near the bottom of your priority list, your marriage is headed for the rocks. You should either move your spouse up your list of priorities or get a divorce.

When considering a divorce, review the status of your marital interactions. If you find that five or more of the situations listed above occur in your marriage, you should contact a divorce counselor or a collaborative divorce attorney immediately—because you likely need a divorce.

Marital Counseling?

An Analysis of the Pros and Cons of Entering Couples Counseling to Save Your Marriage

Successful marriage counseling depends on several factors: both parties must be willing to change, marital problems can't be impossible to fix, your goals need to be realistic, the counselor must be effective, you can't wait until it's too late to begin counseling, and both spouses must want the marriage to work.

Are You Both Willing to Change?

If your partner refuses to attend couples counseling or is unwilling to make any changes in his or her behavior because "it's all your fault," it's nearly impossible to fix your marriage. You may be able to change the dynamics of your relationship by attending individual counseling, but if your spouse is unwilling to make any changes because he or she believes you are causing all the problems, marital counseling is unlikely to work. Marriage problems are rarely one-sided, because both parties usually contribute to a dysfunctional relationship. If only one partner is motivated to change, marital counseling rarely works. However, individual counseling can help the motivated person decide if he or she wants a divorce or can remain in the current relationship.

How Difficult Are Your Problems?

Couples counseling won't fix every marriage. In fact, marriage counseling may lead to divorce if a couple discovers they are in a dysfunctional relationship and can't or won't change their destructive dynamics. About a quarter of couples find their relationship is worse after counseling (usually because only one partner wanted to save the marriage), and over 40 percent of couples who enter marital counseling divorce within four years. Many persons who enter individual counseling discover they developed a dysfunctional attachment to their own parents and carried those destructive patterns into their marriage. Further counseling may repair the dysfunctional attachment relations and help the marriage. However, both spouses must want to change to fix a dysfunctional relationship.

Do You Have Realistic Expectations?

Identifying and working toward realistic goals makes marriage counseling more likely to succeed. For example, if your goal is to improve communications, that's realistic and can probably be achieved. However, if you expect to develop a perfect marital relationship with no conflict, you will be disappointed. Studies show that couples who avoid conflict can't resolve their disputes, develop dysfunctional marriages, and often divorce. Disagreement and anger are natural aspects of marriage. Learning how to handle disagreements through compromise is essential for a happy marriage.

Is Your Counselor Effective?

There are many different therapies available for troubled couples. Different therapeutic techniques work better for different couples. A competent marital counselor will help spouses change the dynamics of their relationship, teach them how to handle conflict, and show them the value of compromise. An effective marital counselor will define and maintain boundaries between the couple to help them approach marriage realistically.

Is It Too Late?

One important fact to remember when evaluating whether couples counseling will work for you is that many couples don't enter counseling until their problems are so bad it's too late to fix the marriage. For counseling to be effective, marital problems must be reasonable, both parties must accept some responsibility for their problems, and both must be willing to change. If the two of you have spent years trying to make your marriage work on your own, you may not have the motivation to participate in serious couples counseling. For marriage counseling to work, you must be willing to experience emotional pain and make significant changes in the way you think and act toward each other. Success depends on both parties being willing to change their behavior.

Among couples who enter marital counseling, about 30 percent of the time, one spouse is already considering divorce. In this situation, the counselor needs to decide whether the goal of counseling is to save the marriage or soften the blow of divorce. If one partner has already decided he or she wants a divorce, there is little point in trying to save the marriage. Only if both partners are willing to work on the marriage will couples counseling work. If your spouse has already decided he or she wants a divorce, you are wasting your time in couples counseling. You should enter divorce counseling or call a collaborative divorce attorney, begin dividing assets, and developing a parenting plan for your children.

Divorce Counseling?

A Discussion of Divorce Counseling as Opposed to Marital Counseling

"Your therapy helped me leave Frank. Frank wants to thank you personally."

When one spouse is considering divorce ("leaning out") while the other spouse wants to save the marriage ("leaning in"), divorce counseling can help the couple decide whether to try couples counseling or see collaborative divorce attorneys. Mixed agendas are common among couples having marital problems. The goal of divorce counseling is to uncover the couple's perceptions of their marriage and help them decide if they want to work on their marriage or end it.

What Is Divorce Counseling?

Divorce counseling is an assessment process rather than marital counseling. It's designed to help couples decide if they want to work on their marriage or get a divorce. When one partner wants to save the marriage and the other is considering divorce, traditional marital counseling rarely works. In fact, counseling a couple with mixed agendas often creates frustration, withdrawal, and dejection because one spouse is committed to working on their problems while the other partner just wants out. Divorce counseling reduces the conflict and confusion between spouses by clarifying their goals and options. A divorce counselor works to understand each spouse's goals for the marriage and his or her individual reasons for wanting to end or save the relationship.

Four Basic Questions

During the initial session, a divorce counselor tries to answer four questions: What caused the marriage problems? What has each spouse done to fix their problems? How do the children factor into the decision to stay married or divorce? What was the best time in the relationship? These questions uncover whether the couple agrees about what caused their problem, clarify whether they are both committed to working on their marriage, indicate how children influence the decision, and explore the shared dreams that brought them together in the first place.

The Partner Who's Leaning Out

During the initial session, a divorce counselor first clarifies how the leaning-out partner feels. Among mixed-agenda college-educated couples considering divorce, around 90 percent of the time it's the wife who wants to end the marriage. If the leaning-out partner has already decided she wants a divorce, the divorce counselor will explore her reasons and find out if she will consider marital counseling. Next, the divorce counselor will explore the leaning-out partner's insight and contribution to the marital dynamic, and determine if he or she believes both spouses contribute to the marital problems or whether he or she believes it's all the other spouse's fault the marriage isn't working.

The Partner Who's Leaning In

Next, the divorce counselor will clarify why the leaning-in partner wants to save the marriage and what he's willing to change to stay married. The divorce counselor will also share information from his partner about why she wants to end the marriage. Often the leaning-in spouse will be in denial about his marital problems and believe everything will work out. The counselor may suggest it's counterproductive to get angry, withdraw, criticize, or beg his spouse to stay married. Instead, the divorce counselor will focus on self-awareness, detail what needs to change in the relationship if it's to survive, and explore what happens if the marriage fails.

Divorce Counseling Clarifies Issues

Divorce counseling is not a waste of time if one partner has definitely decided he or she wants a divorce and has no desire to enter marital counseling. In this case, the counselor can help the leaning-in spouse, who wants to save the marriage, understand the situation he or she faces and help him or her move from denial to a more realistic attitude toward the impending divorce. In those cases where the couple decides to work on their marriage, the counselor will ask each spouse to list the changes they are willing to make to salvage their relationship. Then the counselor will begin marital counseling or refer the couple to another marriage counselor. If the couple decides to divorce, the divorce counselor will suggest behaviors for making the divorce more constructive, such as putting the children's needs first, being respectful of each other, and engaging collaborative divorce attorneys.

Studies show that couples who participate in divorce counseling split approximately equally between those who attempt to reconcile and those who opt for divorce. Among the 50 percent of couples in divorce counseling who try to fix their marriage, an additional 15 percent eventually divorce. This means that about 35 percent of couples who enter divorce counseling stay married, while the other 65 percent get a divorce.

Divorce or Stay?

A Discussion of Deciding to Divorce or Trying to Fix Your Marriage

Getting a divorce is a big step, and few people know how to make the choice intelligently. None of us likes uncertainty, so we put off the decision or make our choice without thinking carefully about options. Procrastination, uncertainty, and second thoughts are natural because there is no guarantee you are making the right choice. The key to making a good decision is to review the pros and cons of your marriage, ask yourself if there is any likelihood both of you can make significant changes, and then base your decision on the balance of the pros and cons and the likelihood of saving the marriage.

Ask these questions: Do you still love your partner? Are you threatening divorce because you're angry or want control of the situation? Are you willing to try marriage counseling? Are you and your spouse willing to change? Do you settle things when you fight? Can you forgive and forget? Do you listen to each other? Are you working toward the same goals? Can you communicate about your feelings? Do you share core values? Do you both feel safe in the marriage? Do you trust each other? Are you having satisfactory sex on a regular basis? If you answered "no" to a majority of these questions, you probably need a divorce. If your reasons for wanting a divorce are unclear, analyze the pluses and minuses of your marriage before making a decision to divorce. Take your time and do it right.

Trial Separation?

When a couple separates, it often means they are headed toward a divorce, but that's not always true. Some couples in marital difficulty need time apart to sort through their feelings and decide whether to stay married or get divorced. Separation does not always mean divorce. It can be a time of renewal, rejuvenation, and reunion. Sometimes being alone can help a person mature and change his or her attitude toward marriage. Couples who choose a marital time-out usually need to see a personal or a marital counselor. Having the courage to let go of the relationship for a short time to gain perspective can give both spouses breathing room and a clearer understanding of their marriage. Other couples use a trial separation as a transition to divorce. For them the separation is a final testing period to make certain divorce is the right decision.

Signs of Good and Bad Marriages

People have five levels of needs: survival, safety, love, esteem, and actualization. If you spend most of the time in your marriage in survival mode, you probably need to end the relationship, but if you live your marriage in the actualization mode, it's fine. If you trust each other, are honest, and can communicate, you most likely have a healthy relationship. If none of these factors is present, your marriage needs work or you need to consider divorce. If you love each other, share interests, and are faithful, you have a good marriage. If not, consider a divorce. If you share mutual respect and are willing to work on your marriage, you have a good chance to stay married. If you feel contempt for each other, share few interests, and are not willing to work on the relationship, you probably need a divorce.

Causes of Divorce

An Analysis of the Major Factors that Cause Most Divorces

Marital problems, such as different core values, substance abuse, sexual problems, financial fights, abuse, or infidelity are serious causes of unhappiness in marriage and often trigger thoughts of divorce. If your marriage involves one or more of these significant issues, you should visit a marriage counselor, an individual therapist, or a collaborative divorce attorney. Even if there is no major problem in your marriage, several minor relationship problems may combine to tip the marital scales toward misery and thoughts of divorce.

Different Core Values

Values differences can create friction, frustration, and anger. For example, if one spouse is religious and the other an atheist, if one is liberal and one conservative, or if one spouse is thrifty while the other likes to spend, these differences can produce serious marital problems. Generally, couples discover whether their values are compatible before marriage, or they learn to live with the differences and decide to marry anyway. However, if one person insists the other party change his or her core values, that's a recipe for divorce.

Substance Abuse

Addiction can destroy a marriage. Although there may be signs of addiction prior to marriage, serious substance abuse often happens years into the marriage. There are only two realistic options for a couple dealing with substance abuse: get professional help for the addicted person or get a divorce. There is little middle ground.

Sexual Dissatisfaction

A frequent complaint among married couples considering divorce is sexual incompatibility. Sometimes couples disagree about how often to have sex and may even drift into a sexless marriage, leaving one spouse frustrated and both unhappy. The constant conflict about whether to have sex can lead to rejection or cold indifference. Because sex is the glue that binds a couple together, when it's missing, the marriage is in danger.

Financial Disagreements

Money difficulties are a frequent source of marital problems. If one partner wants to save money while the other wants to spend it, that can lead to serious marital issues. Additionally, if one partner is accustomed to a higher standard of living than their income will allow, that can produce marital difficulties. Finally, losing a job, suffering an investment loss, or gambling can create serious financial issues. Good money management and agreement about financial goals are important in making a marriage work.

Abuse

Physical, emotional, or sexual abuse are significant causes of divorce. Most patterns of abuse are acquired during childhood. If the person does not seek counseling to deal with his or her own abuse, the same destructive behavior may be reenacted on the next generation. Physical abuse is generally motivated by a need to control the spouse, while sexual abuse is caused by a perversion of normal sexual drive. Finally, emotional abusers are generally reenacting patterns of behavior experienced during childhood.

Infidelity

Adultery can trigger a divorce. Sometimes couples reconcile and rebuild mutual trust, but it's difficult to forgive and forget after an affair. More often, the hurt and anger generated by discovering your spouse has been having sex with someone else is just too damaging, and the only recourse is a divorce. If a couple wants to try rebuilding lost trust, they need to realize it may take eighteen months or more to forgive and forget adultery. Don't expect a quick fix, and do expect lots of anger and recrimination.

Lack of Communication

If a couple can't communicate about their feelings, they will have difficulties adjusting to the minor problems inherent in marriage. It's critical that a couple learn to share feelings, or they will drift apart and find they have little in common.

Minor Causes of Divorce

Other sources of marital difficulty include disagreement about child rearing, feeling controlled, and indifference. Different expectations about who should be responsible for various child-rearing tasks can be a source of problems for a young couple. Feeling manipulated can produce unhappiness and thoughts of divorce. Finally, being bored can happen to couples after years of marriage, as they drift apart and no longer share common interests. "Gray divorce" is on the rise because the children are gone, the spouses may have retired or stopped acquiring new interests and drifted apart. Eventually, as they grow distant and uninterested in each other, these older couples often consider separation or divorce.

No matter whether there is a single major event, such as infidelity, or several minor problems, such as lack of respect, feeling controlled, or disagreements about how to raise the children, marital disputes that don't get resolved by discussion and compromise can grow until they overwhelm the marriage and lead to a divorce.

Causes of Gray Divorce

Causes of Divorce among Older Couples

While the overall divorce rate among all Americans has dropped slightly over the last twenty years, the divorce rate among older Americans has doubled. Couples over age sixty-five have a higher divorce rate than those between fifty and sixty-five. More than one-quarter of current American divorces involve couples over fifty. Older Americans used to enjoy lower divorce rates compared with younger couples, but today, older Americans are divorcing at about the same rate as the general population—and it isn't just older couples in their second or third marriage who are divorcing. More than half of all gray divorces involve a first marriage, and more than 55 percent of gray divorces happen after more than twenty years of marriage. What's causing this spike in gray divorces?

Discord Is Not a Major Reason

Surprisingly, the majority of gray divorces are not marked by serious discord between the couple. Instead, older divorcing couples report they simply drifted apart and one spouse decided he or she wanted a divorce. Researchers are not certain why older Americans are increasingly turning to divorce and why most of these divorces are initiated by women, but they have some ideas.

Women's Expectations Have Changed

One theory is that women's expectations for marriage have changed in the last twenty years. Women now want their partner to be their best friend and their marriage relationship to be a major source of happiness. When their spouse cannot fulfill these heightened expectations, they divorce him and either live alone or remarry.

Women Are Better Educated

Another possible cause of gray divorce is that today, many more women are educated, financially independent, and crave autonomy. Older educated women often decide to get a divorce because their children are grown, they don't have much in common with their spouse, they can expect to live at least another twenty years, and they can afford to live alone and be happy.

Women Have More Options

Older educated women have more options today with online dating sites specifically designed for them and the stigma of cohabitation largely a thing of the past. Older women no longer need to stay married because the alternative is social rejection and poverty. To a lesser extent, the same is true of divorced husbands. A gray divorce isn't the end of the world for older men either. They have productive years ahead, there are plenty of opportunities to meet older single women, and with the right attitude, they can enjoy freedom and fulfillment after a divorce. I went through a gray divorce after forty years of marriage, and I can personally verify there is a good life to be had post-divorce.

Health Is a Critical Factor

For men or women in good health with adequate financial resources, a gray divorce can mean freedom, independence, and personal fulfillment. However, for older men or women in poor health or with limited resources, a gray divorce can force them into poverty. The average older divorced woman has only 20 percent of the net assets owned by a married couple of the same age. In contrast, women who were widowed after age fifty possess more than double the wealth of the average gray divorcee, which makes sense because these widows didn't have to share their assets with a divorced husband.

Infidelity Is Another Cause

Another cause of gray divorce is adultery. The sense of betrayal when someone finds his or her spouse has been cheating with another person can be overwhelming. Many older Americans are facing this difficult emotional upheaval with courage and emerging from a collaborative divorce with a new sense of worth, but the shock and transition can be difficult, and many can't forgive and forget infidelity.

Negative Impact on Older Children

A potential downside to the increase in gray divorces is their negative impact on adult children. Parents usually assume their adult children won't be harmed by a divorce, the way younger children might have been. However, that's not the case; adult children are simply subjected to different emotional stresses, including being used as a sounding board, hearing about their parents' dating, and worrying about them being alone after the divorce. Even if adult children don't take sides, they may have difficulty maintaining proper boundaries because their parents want the older children to be friends and confidants. Putting adult children in these difficult situations can cause serious family discord and personal stresses for the adult children.

The growth in gray divorce presents a unique challenge for

collaborative divorce professionals. Older couples are especially suited to a collaborative divorce because they are mature, have significant assets, and usually want to maintain good relationships with their adult children post-divorce. To this end, the collaborative divorce process offers their best hope of maintaining a close relationship with adult children and avoiding the estrangement so often seen among litigated divorced couples and their families.

Preparing for Divorce

Suggestions on How to Get Ready for a Divorce

Getting a divorce is one of the most painful and costly processes you will ever endure. To avoid being overwhelmed, it helps to plan ahead and get prepared before contacting an attorney and filing for divorce. This chapter will guide you through the preliminary steps to prepare for your divorce.

Do You Really Need a Divorce?

Your first task in preparing for a divorce is to make certain that's what you want. You should probably discuss marriage counseling with your spouse before seeing a divorce attorney. If he or she refuses to visit a marriage counselor, that's a sign you probably need a divorce. You might consider meeting individually with a counselor to discuss getting a divorce. Don't file for divorce until you are really sure you want to end your marriage. Once you make the decision to divorce, meet with a divorce counselor to deal with separating or call a collaborative divorce attorney.

Litigation or a Collaborative Divorce?

Once you decide divorce is in your future, you need to choose between litigation or a collaborative divorce. If you or your partner can't compromise, are dishonest, or one of you wants his or her day in court, you probably need a litigated divorce. On the other hand, if you want a divorce with privacy, dignity, and personal control of the outcome—one that will preserve your family relationships and protect your children, you should choose a collaborative divorce.

Protect Your Children

No matter how angry you feel toward your spouse, don't involve the children in your divorce, and don't badmouth your spouse in front of them. The last thing your children need when their parents are going through a divorce is to be put in the middle. You are more likely to involve your children in your divorce if you go to court, so consider a collaborative divorce if you want to protect them from the worst stresses of divorce.

Collect and Copy Financial Documents

Make copies of the last three years' tax returns, all bank statements, brokerage accounts, insurance policies, mortgage and other loan information, retirement accounts, and credit reports. Copy the deed to your house and the titles to your vehicles, and list all significant personal property such as coins, gun collections, antique furniture, or jewelry. Take pictures of valuable items if you can do this privately. If there is a family business, collect copies of tax returns and financial statements from the business for the last three years. Make copies of any pay slips and employment contracts. Finally, make an inventory of the personal property in your home.

Develop a Budget

List where all the money is spent in your household. Include utilities, food, mortgage, car expenses, medical and dental bills, clothing, entertainment, health insurance, and tuition if your children are in private schools. Once you have compiled a budget for the combined household, estimate what it will cost you to live alone. This may include buying a new home, new furniture, and household items, plus all the usual expenses of running a household. Make your budget realistic so you will actually be able to live within it once you are divorced and on your own.

Protect Your Privacy

You need to plan for an independent life after the divorce by protecting your privacy. Rent a safe-deposit box at a new bank, and store your important papers in it. Rent a post office box so you have a private place to receive confidential mail. Change the passwords on your computer and phone so your spouse can't access those devices.

Start Accumulating Money

Open separate checking and savings accounts at a different bank than the one you and your spouse currently use. When you see your attorney, ask him or her if it's okay to withdraw half the funds from all joint accounts and place them in the new separate checking accounts so you have access to cash. If you don't have an individual credit card, open one in your name so you begin establishing your own separate credit history.

Protect Your Separate Assets

If you inherited funds from your family, received assets as a gift, or collected a personal-injury claim, make certain you keep those assets in an account separate from your joint marital accounts. If you commingle separate funds with community assets, it will be more difficult to prove they are your separate property.

If you decide on a collaborative divorce, ask family, friends, therapists, financial advisors, and business associates for recommendations of a competent attorney. Even if they don't know a competent collaborative divorce attorney, they may know lawyers who can give you reliable recommendations. Another excellent source of information about collaborative divorce attorneys is the Collaborative Divorce Texas website. The site lists well-trained divorce professionals committed to the collaborative process in your area.

How to Get Your Spouse out of the House

A Discussion of Who Should Move out of the House during a Divorce

"I want my spouse out of our house—what should I do?" That's a frequent question I hear in my collaborative divorce practice. Unless there is good evidence of family violence, it's difficult to force a spouse out of the house. There are several factors you and your spouse should consider when deciding who goes and who stays in the home. The first question is, who owns the house? Next, are there children involved? Third, does one of you want to keep the family home after the divorce? Also, who wants the divorce? Finally, does either of you want to date while the divorce is pending? Answers to these questions will help you decide who should leave the family home and who should remain in it.

Who Owns the House?

If the home is community property and there is no evidence of violence, you can't legally force your spouse to move out. On the other hand, if the house is your separate property, you might decide to change the locks on the house and keep your spouse out. However, this tactic will lead to mistrust, anger, and potential litigation, so I don't recommend it. It's better to negotiate an agreement for one of you to leave the home.

Are Children Involved?

If you have children, you and your spouse should try to negotiate temporary custody arrangements for the children. If the mother is going to have primary custody of the children, while the father has visitation rights, then it might make sense for her to stay in the family home with the children while the father moves out. This arrangement will allow the children to stay in a familiar home, go to their regular school, and continue to see their friends. The father can pick up his children for regular visits. The father's apartment or new home should be large enough for the children to stay over and close enough to make transferring them feasible. If you both own the home and there are no children, then other factors may help you decide who moves out while the divorce is pending.

Does One of You Want to Keep the Home?

If one of you wants to keep the house after the divorce and he or she is financially able to afford it, then it makes sense for that person to remain in the home and take it as part of the divorce settlement. On the other hand, if neither of you wants to keep the house after the divorce and there are no children, then it makes little difference who stays in the house. You might decide to live together while the divorce is pending—that's the least expensive option. If you decide that arrangement won't work, then one of you needs to move out while you put the home on the market.

Who Wants the Divorce?

If you want the divorce and there are no children, you are in a difficult position trying to move your spouse out of the family home. Because wives initiate most divorces, the husband may not want the divorce and may refuse to leave his home. Unless you expect to have primary custody of the children or you own the house, it's difficult to force him out. The best tactic in this case is to negotiate an agreement with your spouse for one of you to move out or agree to live together while the divorce is pending.

Do You Want to Date During the Divorce?

If one of you wants to date before the divorce is final, he or she must move out of the house. It's difficult enough dating while you are still married, but imagine the problems involved in dating while you are living in the same home with your spouse. That never works. So, if you want to date, move out.

Getting a spouse out of the house can be difficult. If there are children, the best tactic is to decide on a parenting plan and allow the spouse with primary custody of the children to stay in the family home, at least until the divorce is final. If there are no children, then other factors determine who moves out. If the house is owned by one party, then he or she should probably stay in the home, or they can live in it together while the divorce is pending, to save money. If one of you wants to keep the house after the divorce, then he or she should probably stay in the home. The party who wants the divorce may decide to just move out to keep the peace. Finally, if one of you wants to begin dating before the divorce is final, he or she should certainly move out.

Getting Divorced Sucks

A Realistic Appraisal of What It's Like to Go through a Divorce

"SOMEDAY, SON, ALL THIS WILL BE YOUR EX-WIFE'S."

Your divorce is going to be unpleasant, whether you opt for litigation or a collaborative divorce. Even if you initiate the divorce and are certain you want out of the marriage, getting a divorce process will still be emotional and stressful. If you are angry and want to punish your spouse, you should probably hire a litigation attorney. You will have your day in court and get to tell the world what a jerk your spouse is. However, don't imagine for one second your time in court will be satisfying. You will be humiliated by your spouse's attorney, and you won't feel vindicated, no matter the outcome. Getting a divorce sucks, but one way to make it less stressful is to choose a collaborative divorce rather than litigation.

Collaborative Divorce

If you want to begin healing before the divorce is finished, choose a collaborative divorce rather than litigation. Guided by an experienced team of professionals, you will do the difficult work of separating your finances and deciding how to co-parent your children, while beginning to make yourself psychologically whole again. You will also be able to develop a healthy new relationship with your ex-spouse, so you can co-parent your children effectively post-divorce. Another benefit of the collaborative divorce is that your children won't be put in the middle of the divorce, as may happen in litigation.

Plan Your Future

Now is the time to begin thinking about what you want your life to look like after the divorce. There are decisions to make immediately, including where to live, what sort of lifestyle you can afford, when to begin dating again (I recommend you wait at least until the divorce is final), and how to recover from the financial damage caused by divorce. Also, think beyond immediate problems, and consider how you want to spend the rest of your life. Is there something you always wanted to do but couldn't because you were married? Now is the time to begin planning to do what you love rather than simply working for a living.

Change Your Life

Make a commitment right now, at the beginning of your divorce, to change your life for the better. Don't allow the pain and trauma of the divorce to get you down. Stay optimistic, and try to understand where you've been (your history) and what you want from life (your aspirations). Some people want to be successful, happy, popular, or rich. Others want to achieve their personal dream and not be bound by the demands and expectations of others. You may need to discuss these issues with a counselor.

Experience Your Feelings

To survive a divorce, you must pay attention to your feelings, including the grief, sadness, and anger that accompanies a divorce. Spend time every day attending to how you feel, and try to discover triggers for your emotions. If you feel lonely, ask yourself if it's because you are afraid or depressed. If you're depressed, is it because you are grieving from the loss of your marriage or because you have repressed your anger? Feeling anxious? Try to discover the causes of your fears by asking what frightens you. Do you feel angry? Is it because you're frustrated and can't get people to do what you want? That's a hopeless goal—the only one you can control is yourself. You need to face your feelings, fears, and fantasies by yourself or with the help of a competent counselor and come to terms with the pain of divorce before you can move on and start a new life.

Your Friends May Disappear

Don't be surprised if some of your friends disappear or take your spouse's side during the divorce. They may have been closer to your spouse, or they may drift away to avoid sharing your pain. Difficult as it may be to see your friends leave, it's for the best. Surround yourself with real friends who care about you. They will be there when you need them and will help you through the misery of divorce. Good friends can give you realistic feedback about how you are doing and help you make sensible choices during this difficult time.

Even if you choose a collaborative divorce and try to deal with your spouse amicably, ending your marriage is going to be painful. Litigation is worse, because the parties demonize their spouse to gain an advantage in dividing assets or managing the children. Either way, your life will change dramatically because you will have to move, your children won't be around as much, and you may lose half your assets. There is no such thing as a good divorce—only difficult and awful ones. You will resolve your grief sooner and settle your dispute more fairly through the collaborative divorce process, but it will still be difficult and painful. Be prepared to face some serious challenges over the course of your divorce.

The Four Stages of Divorce

A Preview of What to Expect during the Stages of Divorce

Couples experience four psychological stages during divorce: deliberation, decision, transition, and healing. However, both spouses rarely experience these four stages at the same time, because one spouse often initiates the divorce, while the other spouse is surprised and may want to preserve the marriage. Until both spouses accept the fact that the divorce is going to happen, progress will be slow and painful.

Deliberation Phase

Deliberation begins when the instigator feels there has been a breakdown of the marriage and starts thinking about a divorce. He or she may begin an affair or rewrite the marital history at this stage. In contrast, the other spouse tends to deny marital problems, avoid thinking about the situation, and may begin to feel anxious or jealous about his or her spouse's changed attitude and behavior. During the deliberation phase, a couple's interactions may show signs of anxiety, quiet deadlock, sexual dysfunction, or angry conflict. This phase may last for a few months or even years before the instigator makes a final decision to divorce.

Decision Phase

Decision time occurs when the instigator (usually the wife) decides to tell her spouse, "I want a divorce." This announcement often brings relief to the instigator, along with guilt or depression triggered by a feeling of failure. During this second stage, the other spouse, who often doesn't want the divorce, will experience shock, denial, disbelief, grief, depression, or anger. The couple's interactions during the decision phase can be quiet withdrawal if the couple has a history of denying and avoiding conflict—or turbulent anger if they have a history of fighting. This stage usually lasts only a few weeks or months because the instigator hires an attorney and moves the spouse out of the house if he or she wants to keep it.

Transition Phase

Transition begins when the couple decides to use the collaborative process to end their marriage or one spouse visits a divorce attorney and begins litigation. The instigator typically experiences anger during this stage, may become emotionally agitated, and often feels sad because the marriage has failed. The spouse who doesn't want the divorce may still be in shock and denial or begin experiencing delayed feelings of anger, sadness, depression, and grief during this transition phase. If the couple chooses to litigate, this transition phase can produce heated court hearings and occasional abuse of the legal system if they are a high-conflict couple. If they enter the collaborative divorce process, the couple often begin healing during this transition phase as they learn better communication skills and respect for each other.

Healing Phase

Healing is the final stage of the divorce process. During a collaborative divorce, the instigator usually withdraws emotional investment in the marriage during this stage and begins planning for his or her future. The other spouse, who is finally beginning to realize that the divorce is really going to happen, begins thinking about what his or her new life will be like. The husband, who didn't want the divorce, may recognize for the first time that ending the marriage may be a good thing for him as well. For couples who select the collaborative process, healing happens during the divorce process. However, in litigated cases, healing doesn't usually begin until the divorce dispute is settled or tried in court. A small percentage of high-conflict litigation cases can degenerate into chronic court fights that last for years and consume time, money, and emotional energy.

Generally, one spouse decides he or she wants a divorce, and the other party often wants to save the marriage by entering marital counseling. The spouse who wants to save the marriage may become withdrawn and despondent when threatened with divorce. Whether the parties choose a collaborative or a litigated divorce, the pace of the divorce will be determined primarily by the spouse who is not ready to accept that the marriage is over. Only when both spouses accept that a divorce is going to happen can they begin healing and reach settlement and resolution of their divorce dispute.

Millennial Divorce

A Discussion of the Unique Problems Facing Young Couples during a Divorce

Millennials are believed to be narcissistic, tech smart, and cautious about relationships. These traits suggest they are self-centered, don't want to rush into marriage, and may not stay married once they tie the knot. Studies do show millennials are marrying later, sometimes cohabiting rather than marrying, experimenting with trial marriages, and divorcing less frequently than earlier generations. What's causing this change, and what do millennials need to know about divorce in Texas?

Millennials Marry Later

Millennials are marrying later because they want financial stability, are too restless to settle down, and want to find the right partner before they do. Since money issues, adultery, and dissatisfaction with one's spouse are major causes of divorce, postponing marriage until these problems are resolved seems sensible. Couples who marry in their late twenties are less likely to divorce than couples who marry at other ages, so perhaps millennials are on the right track.

Cohabitation and Divorce

Millennials often live together for years prior to marriage. This is a significant change from earlier generations. Only 10 percent of women who married for the first time between 1965 and 1974 cohabited prior to marriage. Today, cohabitation is the preferred path to marriage for millennial couples. Perhaps cohabitation alerts couples who aren't compatible to break up, and that's why millennials have a lower divorce rate than their parents. However, it's probably not the only reason their divorce rate is lower than earlier generations.

Trial Marriage

Trial or "beta" marriage is an idea borrowed from computer science, where engineers test their products using selected consumers before releasing the computer program to the public. Millennials have applied the idea of beta testing to relationships by contracting for a two-year trial marriage as an alternative to formal marriage. Over 40 percent of millennials support the idea of a trial marriage for two years, after which the terms of marriage could be renegotiated or dissolved without undue formality. Millennials believe that life is a work in progress and they should be able to make changes as they mature. Millennials who cohabit or contract for beta marriages should consider a collaborative divorce if the arrangement doesn't succeed, especially if they have children or significant shared property.

Women Are More Independent

A generation ago, only about 14 percent of women finished college; today over 36 percent of women are college graduates. This means women have more opportunities for employment, are more independent, and face fewer economic pressures to marry than earlier generations. Women today wait longer to tie the knot, and they more often marry for love rather than economic support. However, if they decide they made a mistake, educated women are quick to file for divorce; they initiate almost 90 percent of divorces among college-educated couples.

There Is Little Stigma to Being Single

A generation ago, older unmarried women were called spinsters and stigmatized for being single. Today, women don't feel the need to marry before a certain age because they might face social rejection otherwise. Modern women can stay single and not feel excluded. This helps explain why millennials are marrying later, cohabiting, or having children of their own and not marrying at all.

Parents' Divorces Influenced Millennials

Approximately half of millennials watched their parents struggle through a difficult divorce, and it changed their views on marriage and divorce. Millennials were often pulled into their parents' divorce by serving as sounding boards and giving emotional support. As a result, they developed a healthy respect for the difficulties associated with divorce and are wary of making a marriage commitment. Instead, millennials cohabit or contract for a trial marriage. When these relationships fail, millennials should consider a collaborative attorney to help them with their divorce issues.

Millennials marry later and less often because they don't feel financially or emotionally prepared to settle down until they become more mature. Many millennials are living together rather than marrying, or contracting for a two-year trial marriage. Modern women have opportunities for employment and face fewer social or economic pressures to marry compared with earlier generations. Young women no longer feel pressure to get married before a certain age or face social isolation and economic stress. Millennials have a healthy respect for divorce from watching their own parents go through the process. Even if millennials are divorcing less often and cohabiting more frequently, they still face many of the same legal, economic, and parenting issues as older couples. Cohabiting couples or spouses in a trial marriage who decide to split have often accumulated significant assets and may have children. If so, they must divide assets, arrange a parenting plan, and handle child-support issues if their marriage doesn't work. Millennial couples who split up need a collaborative divorce attorney as much as their older parents did.

Being Realistic about Divorce

How to Think and Act Rationally during a Divorce

A huge problem for divorcing couples is unrealistic expectations about the likely outcome of a divorce, whether they decide on litigation or a collaborative divorce. No matter how couples resolve their marital issues, the experience will be painful. There is no such thing as an easy, friendly divorce. The person who wants a divorce ("the instigator") has usually been unhappy for some time, and he or she finally decides to end the marriage. The person who wants to maintain the marriage ("the divorcee") has probably been in denial for months but will wake up when his or her spouse requests a divorce. No matter whether you wanted the divorce or not, both parties will feel pain at different times and in different ways during the course of ending the marriage. You can minimize the pain by managing expectations and choosing a collaborative divorce, but the process will still be stressful and difficult.

There Are No Winners in Divorce

Many people believe they can win when they go through a divorce, but that's rarely true. There are usually two losers. You must divide your marital estate in an equitable manner, so both of you will have less money for everyday living expenses after the divorce. As a result, you may have to change your lifestyle and standard of living to make ends meet. You may have to move to a smaller home, and you will probably share custody of your children. Change is always difficult, but so much dislocation at one time can be frightening and overwhelming. However, if you face facts realistically and keep your anger under control, you can survive a divorce. It won't be easy, though.

Being Innocent Doesn't Help

It's a common belief that the courts will favor an "innocent" spouse and punish the one who is at "fault." That's not really correct—Texas is a no-fault divorce state, which means the courts don't really care who asked for the divorce or who is at fault. Fault can be used as a factor in dividing assets, but it rarely makes more than a 5 percent difference in allocating the marital estate. However, if one parent is abusive, he or she may face supervised visits with the children and be ordered to pay spousal maintenance.

Communicating Can Save Money

If you hire a litigation attorney, one of the first things he or she will say is, "Don't talk to your spouse about anything—let me talk to his or her attorney." On the other hand, if you choose a collaborative divorce, you will be able to communicate with your spouse and meet with him or her on a regular basis during joint collaborative meetings. This open communication fosters trust, better co-parenting, and a quicker resolution of the dispute. It's also helpful for children to see that their parents can communicate and work together during the divorce. Communicating can save you time and money in reaching a settlement and preserve your parenting relationship with the children.

Emotions Run High During Divorce

Don't expect to remain calm during a divorce. You will feel sad, anxious, and angry. However, if your emotions seem to be getting out of control or are overwhelming you, see a counselor to help you deal with your feelings and discover the triggers for your strong emotions. It's better to deal with these emotions in counseling rather than venting in court, at your collaborative attorney's office, or during the joint collaborative meetings. Don't expect your children to behave normally during the divorce either, because they have emotional reactions to all the changes that are happening. The children may withdraw, act out, have difficulties at school, or have trouble sleeping. Counseling can help them as well.

Finally, don't expect your divorce to be finished in a month. Texas requires a sixty-day waiting period before a couple can divorce, and it usually takes longer to complete discovery, negotiations, settlement, and drafting of the Divorce Decree and Agreement Incident to Divorce. Expect the process to take from three to six or seven months. I always tell my collaborative clients that "fighting costs extra," and after one or two joint meetings, they begin to understand and learn to control their emotions so they can save money and time. Also, a neutral mental-health professional can help both spouses learn to communicate and interact in a more effective manner. No matter whether you choose litigation or a collaborative divorce, realistic expectations will help make the process easier, faster, and less expensive.

Coping with Loss

Psychological Advice about How to Deal with the Grief Caused by a Divorce

Your spouse steps into the living room and says, "We need to talk." Immediately, your stress level goes sky-high, and you begin to feel defensive. However, you can't avoid the issue, so you face the music and agree to talk. After a few preliminary comments about how unhappy she has been for the past several months, your wife tells you, "I don't want to be married to you anymore. I have hired an attorney, and she will be sending you papers later this week. I want you out of the house as soon as you find an apartment."

Has something like that happened to you recently, or have you said that to your spouse? If so, you know how awful it feels for both parties. This chapter will discuss loss, primarily from the viewpoint of the spouse who wants to save the marriage, but the feelings of loss and grief are common to both.

You Are Shocked

Sure, you've been vaguely aware your spouse was unhappy and withdrawn the last few months, but you attributed that to her father's recent death, and you never dreamed she was thinking about divorce. Now, you realize you missed something important, and it may be too late to save your marriage. You decide to give it a try anyway, so you ask, "Can we work this out? How about marital counseling? You have said you wanted to do that in the past." Your spouse says, "No, it's too late. I want a divorce."

Denying the Problem

Your immediate reaction is probably to slip into denial. You think to yourself, *She's just upset about something, and when she calms down, everything will be fine.* However, denying you have a serious problem won't help, and avoiding thinking about the anxiety, anger, and depression caused by your wife's threat of divorce will make matters worse. Everyone is vulnerable to stress and grief when faced with a serious loss such as divorce or death. If you're feeling overwhelmed, seek counseling. Avoiding feeling the stress and grief associated with a divorce will make matters worse. To get through the loss, you need to allow yourself to experience the sadness, anger, and fear. Focusing on positive things in your life will help. Stay in touch with family and friends, and avoid isolation. It's okay to feel sorry for yourself, but don't become passive. Be proactive and take charge of the situation instead of becoming depressed.

Emotional Problems during Divorce

The most frequent emotional problems associated with divorce are anger, anxiety, depression, and substance abuse. There are healthy steps you can take to deal with feelings of grief. An important factor in achieving emotional stability during a divorce is to maintain some sense of control over your life and avoid feeling like a victim. Being active will give you a sense of achievement. Additionally, it's important to eat right, exercise, and maintain a positive mental attitude. Meditate or do relaxation exercises regularly and take care of yourself.

Dealing with Stress

Exercise and stress management are essential components of emotional health during a divorce. Daily exercise is an effective way to modulate mood, dissipate stress, and relieve depression. Also, it helps to spend time relaxing and breathing deeply. Gradually increase your walking or running, to relieve depression and gain energy. Try to replace alcohol or drugs with a safer way to relax. Pay attention to your surroundings. Psychologists call this state *mindfulness*—being aware of yourself in your world. However, old habits are difficult to change. Take inventory of your life, and ask yourself which habits make life difficult for you. The key is to focus on things that are important to you and plan positive activities for your future. Life is not over, even though it may seem that way at the moment.

Don't expect your grief and anger to go away quickly. It may take six or eight months for you to feel more or less normal, and even then, you will likely have recurring short bouts of sadness when reminded of your loss. The important thing is to experience your grief when it occurs, work through it, and come out the other side of the divorce stronger and happier. Avoid negative people. Choose friends and activities that make you feel better. Think positive, stay proactive, avoid being isolated, and choose a collaborative divorce. The collaborative team will teach you how to communicate, compromise, and connect with your spouse and family after the divorce. You and your children will be better off as a result.

Educated Women File Most Divorces

A Discussion of Why Most Divorces Are Initiated by Educated Women

Because single mothers generally have financial problems, it's commonly assumed that husbands initiate most divorces. However, that's not true. Throughout history, American women have filed the vast majority of divorces. Approximately 75 percent of all divorces are initiated by wives, while 90 percent of divorces among college-educated couples are filed by women. Studies show women's standard of living falls following a divorce. So, why are college-educated women filing for divorce so often? There are several likely reasons.

Marital Isolation

Some educated women report they filed for divorce because they felt neglected by their husbands and unhappy in their marriage. These women say their husbands were indifferent, didn't communicate, and neglected their feelings. They also said they felt isolated in their marriage and needed a divorce to develop their own life and gain personal autonomy. These women felt marriage inhibited their individual growth, lacked intimacy, and caused them to be unhappy. However, recent studies show that social isolation is not the main reason college-educated women initiate most divorces.

Emotional or Physical Abuse

Another possible reason women file for divorce is to escape an abusive relationship. To find out, two economists studied forty-six thousand divorces in Connecticut, Virginia, Montana, and Oregon that were filed during 1995. They asked whether abuse was a major reason college-educated women file for divorce. The state with the best records, Virginia, showed only 6 percent of divorces were granted on grounds of abuse. Adultery, another form of abuse, was alleged as often by husbands as wives in Virginia, so that wouldn't explain why 90 percent of divorces were filed by college-educated women. Marital abuse and infidelity apparently are not the major reasons college-educated women initiate most divorces.

Being Better Educated

Another incentive to divorce is the belief that your partner is not good enough for you. Women might be tempted to leave men who are not well educated or economically successful, particularly if the woman is college educated and financially independent. Economists found that better-educated spouses are more likely to initiate a divorce in the four states they studied. However, better education and financial success for women accounted for only a small percentage of the divorces and would not explain why women initiate 90 percent of divorces among college-educated couples in these four states.

Child Custody

Surprisingly, the factor that explains why 90 percent of divorces among college-educated couples are initiated by women involves who gets primary custody of the children. This is particularly true when there is no significant dispute about property or when the couple had been separated before the divorce was filed. College-educated women in the four states studied initiated 90 percent of divorces primarily because they believed they would be awarded custody of their children, they would receive child-support payments, and their husbands would be ordered to pay alimony. For women, children are the most important asset in the marriage, and educated wives initiate divorce to gain control of their children and receive child support and alimony.

In most states, mothers have historically been awarded sole or primary custody of their children, and their husbands were given visitation rights and ordered to pay child support and alimony. Having custody of the children and receiving financial support from their ex-husbands gave wives the power to make all the important decisions concerning their children's welfare, while receiving financial support from their ex-husbands during the time they were caring for the children. Initiating divorce to gain custody of children and receive financial support gave women significant parental and financial power. If states were to change this incentive and mandate joint custody as the preferred arrangement for parents, fathers would be more likely to nurture their children, and women would be less likely to initiate divorce as a way to gain power over their husbands, control of their children, and child-support payments. Recently, several states, including Texas, have made joint custody the presumptive norm because they want to encourage co-parenting of children. This change toward joint custody may explain part of the recent decline in divorce rates among younger Americans.

Litigated or Collaborative Divorce?

The Pros and Cons of Litigation and the Collaborative Process

"I thought your wife wasn't contesting the divorce."

There are two ways to divorce in Texas: litigation or a collaborative divorce. In a collaborative divorce, you control the outcome, your goals and interests are taken seriously during negotiations, financial information is shared openly, you help negotiate a win-win settlement, you avoid harm to your children, you don't go to court, and you save money. In a litigated divorce, the attorneys control the case, your goals and interests may be decided by the court, information is often hidden, each side attempts to win, the children may be placed in the middle, and litigation costs more on average than a collaborative divorce.

The Collaborative Process

During the first joint meeting, two attorneys, a neutral financial professional, and a neutral mental-health professional explain the collaborative process, review expectations of conduct, discuss the family law participation agreement, and help clients develop goals and interests. The parties sign the participation agreement, and the financial professional discusses the information needed to develop settlement options.

Settlement Options

During the next few meetings, the collaborative team and parties review financial information, discuss goals and interests of each party, identify issues, create settlement options, and compare each option with the clients' goals and interests. The team eliminates settlement options that don't meet both clients' goals and interests and begin to narrow issues for settlement.

Negotiate Settlement and Draft Documents

During the last few collaborative meetings, the team and parties negotiate a collaborative settlement agreement and sign it. Following settlement, the attorneys draft a Divorce Decree and Agreement Incident to Divorce. Once the closing documents are complete, one attorney and his client will prove up the divorce before a judge; this only takes a few minutes and is not stressful.

The Litigation Process

The first step in a litigated divorce is to file an original petition and serve it on the other side. Even if both parties agree they want a divorce, a petition must be filed stating the grounds for divorce (usually incompatibility) or alleging fault (abuse, adultery, or abandonment). The petition is usually served on the spouse's attorney, but the sheriff may show up at a spouse's workplace and embarrass him or her if the parties are especially angry.

Response and Temporary Orders

The served spouse must file a response to the petition, usually a general denial. However, if there are allegations of fault, the response should rebut the facts of the petition connected with the allegations of fault and raise all relevant defenses. Next comes a temporary hearing before a judge, to decide where the children will live during the divorce, establish a visitation schedule until final settlement or trial of the case, and determine how much temporary support and child support will be paid by whom.

Discovery Issues

Following the temporary hearing, attorneys exchange formal requests for discovery and may schedule oral depositions of witnesses and the parties. Discovery disputes can consume substantial time and money if the issues are complex, the parties disagree, and the attorneys try to hide information. Attorneys will ask the court to settle discovery disputes that cannot be negotiated satisfactorily. Discovery issues are a major cause of delay and additional costs during litigation.

Settlement Negotiations

Once discovery is complete, the attorneys may agree to meet for settlement negotiations, or the court may order the parties to mediation, in an effort to settle the dispute. About 85 percent of litigated cases settle at this point. If the parties disagree about custody, the court may order a social study to determine which parent should receive primary custody of the children, and the issue may have to be decided by a jury at trial.

Trial

If the parties are unable to settle their dispute, the court will set the case for trial before a judge or jury. At trial, both parties make opening statements, present and cross-examine witnesses, introduce evidence, and make closing arguments. Then, the judge or jury decides the issues, including who will have custody of the children (a jury question), how the marital estate will be divided, the amount of child support, and whether spousal support is justified (judicial decisions). Finally, the attorneys will draft the Divorce Decree and Agreement Incident to Divorce and take one party to court to prove up the divorce.

The advantages of a collaborative divorce are privacy, lower cost, flexibility of scheduling, control of the process, custom settlement solutions, protection of the children, and better post-divorce co-parenting. The advantages of a litigated divorce are that discovery can be ordered by the court if one party refuses to disclose information, protective orders are available in cases of physical abuse, and the court can resolve the dispute if the parties can't compromise. Which type of divorce is best for you depends on your goals, interests, and level of anger.

The Best Way to Divorce in Texas

A Discussion of Why Choosing a Collaborative Divorce Is Best for Your Family

What's the best way to divorce? You can choose either a collaborative divorce or litigation. A collaborative divorce offers many benefits, including privacy, lower cost, transparency, client control of the outcome, convenient scheduling, preserving family relationships, protecting children, allowing creative settlement solutions, and minimizing post-divorce conflicts. In a litigated divorce, the benefits include court-ordered discovery, a restraining order against family violence, and a court-ordered settlement if you can't agree. Many couples find the benefits of a collaborative divorce compelling. The best way to divorce depends on your goals, interests, and emotions. If you want your day in court, choose litigation. However, if you prefer to avoid fighting, want to maintain good relations with your co-parent after the divorce, and protect your children, you should opt for a collaborative divorce; it has many benefits.

Privacy

Communications and documents produced during a collaborative divorce are confidential. This means none of the collaborative team can be compelled to testify about what happened during a collaborative divorce, and no document can be disclosed for use during trail. In contrast, in a litigated divorce, everything is public and subject to discovery. Professionals who want to protect their reputation, wealthy individuals who want to keep their estate private, and anyone who has committed an indiscretion, such as adultery, will appreciate the benefit of keeping their personal life out of the courtroom by choosing a collaborative divorce.

Lower Cost

In Texas, the average cost of a collaborative divorce is lower than the average cost of a litigated divorce. Using only two attorneys, rather than a full team including a financial professional and a mental-health professional, costs less and is appropriate for cases with no children and simple finances. Costs vary by complexity of the case and cooperativeness of the clients. This means clients who choose a collaborative divorce preserve assets for the family rather than giving them to attorneys.

Transparency

Participants in the collaborative process voluntarily agree to produce all relevant financial and family information, so there's less worry about hidden assets. The collaborative parties often sign an affidavit stating they have fully disclosed all marital property. Moreover, collaborative financial professionals are trained to analyze financial information and detect missing data. In contrast, litigation attorneys generally try to hide documents and force the other side to submit formal discovery requests to uncover assets. It's less likely your spouse is hiding assets if he or she agrees to a collaborative divorce rather than litigation.

Client Control of the Outcome

A collaborative divorce is settled through interest-based negotiation, so clients control the outcome and don't turn their future over to a judge or jury. A litigated divorce is controlled by attorneys and the court. Do you prefer to be in control of your divorce, or do you want attorneys and a judge to determine your future and the future of your children?

Convenience

Collaborative meetings are scheduled at the convenience of the parties, which is a real advantage for busy professionals who can't easily take time from work to attend lengthy hearings scheduled at the convenience of the court and attorneys.

Preserving Family Relationships

The collaborative process helps divorcing couples communicate and work together to reach a settlement. In contrast, a litigated divorce brings out the worst in people, makes them hate each other, and may destroy any chance they have to work together post-divorce. In litigation, the children may be dragged into the middle of their parents' litigated divorce through a custody dispute.

Protecting Children

Children aren't put in the middle of a collaborative divorce. If the collaborative team needs information about the children, a child specialist is engaged to interview them and produce a report. In a litigated divorce, children may be forced to meet with the judge in chambers to tell the court where they want to live after the divorce is final.

Creative Settlements

The collaborative process allows clients and their attorneys to reach creative settlements that may not be available in court. Collaborative settlements can produce shared custody, out-of-guideline child support, contractual alimony to take advantage of differing spousal tax rates, and unusual divisions of the community estate.

Minimizes Post-Divorce Conflicts

Parties who participate in a collaborative divorce learn how to communicate, respect each other, and discover that fighting is not productive. Collaborative couples are able to co-parent more effectively after the divorce, compared with parents who choose litigation. Many litigated divorces end up back in court to resolve disputes that could be worked out between the parties if they were reasonable.

For clients who want to avoid stress, save money, and maintain good relations with their family after the divorce, the best way to divorce in Texas is through the collaborative process. You should seriously consider a collaborative divorce rather than litigation if you are untying the knot. You and your children will be better off, it won't cost as much as a litigated divorce, and you will be better co-parents when it's over.

Confidentiality and Disclosure

The Benefits of Privacy and Transparency in a Collaborative Divorce

Confidentiality and disclosure are two important reasons for choosing a collaborative divorce. Ordinarily, legal confidentiality covers only direct communications between an attorney and his or her client. However, within a collaborative divorce, all communications are confidential. In contrast, a litigated divorce is open to the public. When the collaborative couple signs the family law participation agreement, they commit to disclose all relevant information. The collaborative parties can be required to sign an affidavit stating they have fairly and fully disclosed all marital property, and a paragraph can be included in the divorce decree awarding any undisclosed marital asset to the party who did not possess or control the property prior to divorce.

Collaborative Confidentiality

Confidentiality of the collaborative process is guaranteed by the Texas Collaborative Family Law Act. Disclosure of collaborative communications is prohibited, so not even a court can demand the disclosure of privileged collaborative information, except under limited circumstances. The Texas Collaborative Family Law Act allows the parties to agree that their conduct during meetings and even communications that occurred before signing the Collaborative Family Law Participation Agreement are confidential.

Limits of Privilege

The Texas Collaborative Family Law Act sets limits on the scope of privilege. Privilege does *not* apply to communications contained in a collaborative settlement agreement in writing and signed by the parties. This means that a signed collaborative settlement agreement *is* discoverable. Additionally, the privilege can be waived if *all* parties and nonparty participants agree. Finally, limits on privilege apply when there has been a threat of bodily harm or a crime, abuse is suspected, or there's a claim of professional misconduct, an allegation of fraud, a dispute about attorney fees, or a claim against a third party who didn't sign the collaborative agreement.

Full Disclosure—The Neutral Financial Professional

Collaborative financial professionals are trained to analyze documents and detect missing assets. By comparing information from tax returns, brokerage firms, banks, employment contracts, pension plans, cash-flow analyses, and net-worth statements, collaborative financial professionals are likely to determine if there are any undisclosed assets. For example, if a tax return shows dividend or interest income, but there is no corresponding brokerage or bank statement showing assets that earned the dividend or interest income, that's an indication that marital assets may be hidden.

Ways to Hide Assets

There are several ways to hide assets that are difficult to uncover, including stashing cash in a safe-deposit box, prepaying income taxes, giving cash to a friend for safekeeping, or depositing funds in a numbered offshore account. It's difficult to discover cash hidden in a safe-deposit box unless you find a clue. You can question your spouse under oath and analyze the books to see if they balance, but these methods are not foolproof. Prepaid income tax is easy to find if you remember to look. Hiding money with a friend or paramour is difficult to discover, even if you take their depositions. Finding money hidden in a numbered offshore account is nearly impossible; even the IRS has difficulty discovering the existence of these accounts.

Why Should I Trust Collaborative Disclosure?

A common question asked by couples considering a collaborative divorce is, "How can I be certain my spouse isn't hiding assets?" It's natural to be concerned that your spouse may be hiding money. However, the collaborative process contains several safeguards to ensure that all assets are disclosed voluntarily. In contrast, there is no assurance of full voluntary disclosure in a litigated divorce. Collaborative attorneys make certain their client discloses all significant information, while litigation attorneys generally hide assets and force the other side to search for them. If a collaborative attorney believes his or her client is hiding assets, the attorney must tell the client to disclose the asset or the collaborative attorney must withdraw from representation. This usually convinces a collaborative client to cooperate. If they don't, the resignation alerts the other side that there is a discovery problem. Litigation attorneys have no such duty.

Professionals with a reputation to protect, wealthy individuals with large estates they wish to keep private, and anyone who has committed an indiscretion (such as marital fraud) will appreciate the benefit of keeping their personal lives out of the courtroom by agreeing to a collaborative divorce. Full disclosure is an added benefit of the collaborative divorce because it gives added assurance there are no hidden assets. Discovery disputes during a litigated divorce are costly and encourage hiding assets, because there is no contractual obligation to disclose relevant information during litigation. In contrast, collaborative clients agree to full disclosure and engage a single neutral financial professional trained to spot missing assets. By agreeing to a collaborative divorce, you and your spouse have agreed not to hide assets and signaled you want an amicable settlement of your dispute without court intervention.

How to Find the Right Divorce Lawyer

A Step-by-Step Guide to Finding the Right Collaborative Lawyer for You

Getting a divorce is complicated and stressful. To navigate the legal process efficiently and avoid costly mistakes, you need to find the right divorce attorney to guide you through the process. First, decide whether you want a collaborative or a litigated divorce. A collaborative divorce is cooperative, less stressful, maintains family relationships, avoids serious damage to your children, saves money, gives you confidentiality, allows client control, and offers flexible scheduling to accommodate busy professionals. However, if you don't trust your spouse, you can't compromise, or you want your day in court, you should choose a litigation attorney. The process of finding either type of divorce attorney is similar.

Reliable Sources of Information

Good sources for recommendations are family, friends, counselors, financial advisors, and business associates. Even if they don't know a collaborative divorce attorney, they may know lawyers who can give you reliable recommendations. An excellent source of information about qualified collaborative divorce attorneys is the Collaborative Divorce Texas website, because well-trained collaborative divorce professionals committed to the process are members of this statewide organization. Look for collaborative attorneys who are credentialed by Collaborative Divorce Texas—their credentialed status will be noted on the website. It's important to make certain the attorney you select is collaboratively trained and credentialed, because many attorneys offer collaborative divorces but are not properly trained or committed to the process. Instead, they advertise collaborative divorce as a bait-and-switch tactic. Dealing with a collaborative divorce attorney is a deeply personal experience, so you will want to interview them to find one who makes you feel comfortable and confident. If you want assurance of a well-trained collaborative attorney, select one who is credentialed by Collaborative Divorce Texas.

Research the Lawyer's Experience

Go online and search the lawyer's website. For example, enter "collaborative divorce San Antonio" into your preferred search engine, and you will find websites for several trained and experienced collaborative divorce lawyers in the San Antonio area. Some collaborative attorneys are credentialed by Collaborative Divorce Texas, which assures they are trained, experienced, and committed to the collaborative process. Change the city to find similar websites in other locations throughout Texas. Select the lawyers recommended to you, or find a collaborative attorney online and review his or her education, experience, training, and legal background. Make sure you find collaborative attorneys who are trained and credentialed in the collaborative divorce process, because they are better trained and more experienced. If you engage a divorce attorney who prefers to do litigation but dabbles in collaborative divorces, you will likely be steered toward the courtroom, even though that may not be your preference.

Check for Complaints

After reviewing collaborative attorneys' websites, noting where they were educated, how long they have been licensed in Texas, and how experienced they are in collaborative divorce, check their professional background with the Texas State Bar Association to make certain they have not received complaints from former clients or had disciplinary actions filed against them. When you have found two or three collaborative attorneys who are qualified and free of problems, call their offices and make appointments to interview them.

Be Prepared

Before you show up at the collaborative lawyer's office, be prepared to tell your story clearly and succinctly. Bring copies of your financial records and an outline of significant events in your marital history to share with the lawyer. This will save time during the interview and help you cover important points.

Ask Questions

Approach the meeting like a job interview, because you are hiring the attorney to work for you. Ask questions to find out what the attorney thinks about your case, and make certain you understand what he or she is saying. Find out how much of the attorney's practice is devoted to collaborative divorce. You don't want to engage an attorney who claims to be collaborative but is primarily a litigation lawyer. Note whether the attorney is organized, if he or she will return your phone calls in a timely manner, and is a good listener. Make certain you understand the attorney-client contract and fee arrangement. Ask yourself if the attorney seems competent, confident, and answers your questions clearly and completely. Most important, do you feel comfortable about this person's skills and personality? You will be spending a lot of time with him or her in difficult, emotional situations, and you must feel good about the relationship.

Select an Organized Attorney

Consider cost in selecting an attorney. This does not mean you should select the attorney with the lowest hourly fee. An experienced attorney with an organized approach will cost less than a cheaper young lawyer with no plan. A collaborative divorce will, on average, cost less than a litigated divorce, and an organized attorney will prepare and settle your collaborative divorce more quickly. Once you choose an attorney, let him or her know right away you want him or her to manage your divorce. Good attorneys are in high demand, so don't delay and miss out on hiring the lawyer who is right for you.

Make certain the details of the attorney-client contract are clear, in writing, and signed by both parties. Pay particular attention to the scope of work offered, the fee arrangement, and how the retainer works, and understand how to communicate with your lawyer. If you follow these simple steps, you will find the right divorce lawyer for you.

Bait-and-Switch Attorneys

A Warning about Attorneys Who Advertise Collaborative Divorce but Only Do Litigation

Some attorneys advertise that they offer collaborative divorce, but when a client comes to their office, the lawyer says a collaborative divorce isn't appropriate and recommends litigation. The "bait" is an ad or website offering collaborative divorce, which is attractive to many clients because it's private, flexible, allows the couple to preserve their co-parenting relationship post-divorce, is less expensive, and protects children from the stress of litigation. The "switch" is to tell clients their case isn't right for collaborative divorce and sign them up for litigation, which is more expensive, stressful, destructive of family relationships, and potentially harmful to children.

How Legal Bait and Switch Works

Bait-and-switch attorneys don't intend to offer a collaborative divorce to their clients. They simply advertise the availability of a collaborative divorce to get clients into their offices, so they can sign them up for litigation. In some cases, there may be legitimate reasons an attorney might recommend litigation, for example, if he or she sees the client's personality would make it nearly impossible for him or her to compromise or voluntarily disclose financial information. The attorney may also discover that the prospective client has unrealistic expectations that the collaborative process will magically save his or her marriage. If there are legitimate reasons for an attorney to recommend a litigated divorce, the attorney should share the reasons with the client immediately rather than simply pressure the client to sign on the dotted line and litigate the divorce. However, that's not what's happening in most of these cases—the bait-and-switch attorney doesn't intend to offer a collaborative divorce, no matter the personality of the client.

Bait-and-Switch Attorneys Aren't Trained in Collaborative Divorce

Often, litigation attorneys who advertise that they do collaborative divorces aren't trained in the collaborative process, they have little commitment to resolve family disputes outside the courthouse, and they don't believe the collaborative process works. Instead, they simply advertise collaborative divorce because more and more people are learning about this new way to divorce with dignity; litigation attorneys want to attract these bright, affluent clients into their practice and switch them to a litigated divorce.

How to Avoid Legal Bait and Switch

There are several things you can do to avoid being the victim of a bait-and-switch litigation attorney. Do your homework. Read the attorney's website and see what he or she says about collaborative divorce. Does the attorney prominently display collaborative divorce on the website? Is he or she trained and credentialed in collaborative divorce? Does the attorney belong to a local professional collaborative practice group and to Collaborative Divorce Texas? Find out how much of the attorney's practice is devoted to collaborative divorces and how much to litigated divorces. There are attorneys who do only collaborative divorces, so if you want to be certain you have an attorney who won't pull a bait and switch on you, engage one who does no litigated divorces. If an attorney does both collaborative and litigated divorces, ask what percentage of his or her divorces are collaborative. If the attorney only does a small number of collaborative divorces, it's possible he or she will bait and switch you.

Attorneys who do only collaborative divorces may practice other types of law, such as real estate or estate planning. If an attorney does no litigation or at least half of his or her divorce practice is collaborative, you can be fairly certain the attorney won't bait and switch you. Finally, when you interview the attorney, pay attention to how much he or she knows about collaborative divorce and how it works. If the attorney doesn't spend time clearly describing the benefits and risks of a collaborative divorce and the benefits and risks of a litigated divorce, he or she is not being honest with you. Attorneys have an ethical obligation to inform you of your divorce options in Texas, including collaborative divorce and litigation. If the bait-and-switch attorney spends little or no time discussing collaborative divorce and almost immediately tells you that a collaborative divorce is not for you, be suspicious. He or she is enticing you to the office with the offer of a collaborative divorce but is selling you litigation, because that will make more money, and he or she may not know how to do a collaborative divorce.

Divorce Myths

Debunking the Top Divorce Myths so You Won't Be Misled

Getting divorced is difficult enough without dealing with misinformation. Here are some common myths about divorce that need to be clarified before you begin your divorce.

Myth 1: Mom Always Gets the Kids

A generation ago, Mom raised the children while Dad worked, so it made sense for her to have custody of the children and Dad to visit them and pay child support. Today, many women are working and men are caring for children, so custody can be shared.

Myth 2: Each Spouse Receives Half the Assets

Equitable division of the marital estate means a fair split of community assets, not necessarily a fifty-fifty split. For example, a mom who has taken care of the children and not worked for years may be awarded a larger share of assets than a wife who holds a medical degree and has a full-time practice.

Myth 3: Divorce Means You Failed

You may feel like a failure because you are getting a divorce. However, it's rare for a divorce to be entirely one person's fault. Not wanting to be married to someone doesn't mean you are a bad person. Personality differences beyond your control cause most divorces.

Myth 4: If We Share Custody, There Will Be No Child Support

In shared-custody cases, if one spouse earns more, the court or couple may decide the higher-earning person should pay the difference between guideline support for both salaries when they share custody.

Myth 5: We Never Married, So We Don't Need a Divorce

If you lived together and told people you were married, you may have a common-law marriage. See an attorney to find out if you are informally married and need a formal divorce. Even if you don't have a common-law marriage, you may have shared assets and children, so you will need to formalize the breakup of your relationship.

Myth 6: Woman Always Get Alimony

In Texas, stay-at-home moms who have no work skills and have been married for ten years or more are generally awarded spousal support for a few years while they finish school or polish job skills. Sometimes, the husband may agree to pay contractual alimony, but it's not automatic in Texas unless you meet statutory guidelines.

Myth 7: You Must File for Divorce Where You Married

You file for divorce where you currently reside, not where you were married. At least one spouse must reside for six months in Texas and for ninety days in the county where the divorce is filed.

Myth 8: You Can Trade Assets for Lower Child Support

Property division and child support are separate issues. Child support is usually awarded according to the children's needs and the parties' ability to pay. Texas has standard child-support guidelines that are presumed to be in the child's best interest.

Myth 9: Older Children Can Choose Where They Want to Live

Texas children over twelve may state a preference for where they want to live after the divorce is final. However, the decision is made by the parents or a judge and doesn't necessarily follow the child's wishes.

Myth 10: My Spouse Can Stop Our Divorce

With no-fault divorce, anyone who wants out of a marriage can leave. This doesn't mean divorce is easy or inexpensive, but you can always end a marriage.

Myth 11: The Engagement Ring Is Marital Property

The engagement ring was a gift from the husband to his wife, so it's her separate property, and she keeps it, unless it's a family heirloom. Then the ring goes back to the family of origin.

Myth 12: No-Fault Makes It Easy for Men to Divorce

Seventy-five percent of Texas divorces are initiated by women, because they are more financially independent, they expect more from a marriage, and they often receive primary custody of the children and child support. Men are not abandoning their spouse due to no-fault divorce.

Myth 13: Divorce Doesn't Harm Children

Children want their family to stay together. Their happiness comes from a home with two parents, a routine, friends, and a good school. Divorce can be difficult for children.

Myth 14: Having Children Preserves a Marriage

There is no difference between the divorce rate of couples with and without children.

Myth 15: It's Okay to Deny Visitation if He's Late Paying Child Support

Visitation and child support are independent rights and duties, and you can't deny him access to your children because he is late paying child support.

Myth 16: The Wife Always Gets the House

Sometimes it makes sense for Mom to keep the family home so the children can stay in their school, see their friends, and feel secure. However, moving may make more financial sense.

Myth 17: Second Marriages Are More Successful

A popular myth is that people learn from their mistakes, so second marriages are more likely to last. In fact, second and third marriages have a higher failure rate than first marriages.

Myth 18: Living Together Makes Divorce Less Likely

You may experience fewer surprises if you live with a person prior to marriage, but couples who live together before marriage still divorce.

Myth 19: Being Single Means You Have More Money

Because you must divide family assets during divorce, and the process itself is costly, it's unlikely you will have more money after the divorce.

Myth 20: Divorce Can Be Inexpensive if You Agree on Everything

Fighting costs extra, so couples can limit the cost of their divorce to some extent by agreeing to a settlement. However, many couples have complex legal, financial, and child issues that must be negotiated or litigated, so most divorces are expensive.

Handling Divorce Fears

How to Deal with Your Worst Fears During a Divorce

Are you in a difficult marriage and afraid to get out? Do you fight with your spouse all the time, think about divorce every day, but are too frightened to act? Feeling depressed and unhappy but afraid to see a collaborative divorce attorney? Do you worry about being alone and broke after a divorce? Are you staying in your marriage because of the kids? If you recognize yourself here, you aren't alone. Everyone feels unhappy in a bad marriage and is anxious about getting a divorce. However, if you want to feel better and improve your life, you must deal with your fears and decide to work on your marriage or get a divorce.

Fear of the Future

We all fear uncertainty. You naturally wonder what life will be like after a divorce. A big fear for many people contemplating divorce is not knowing what will happen after it's over: where will I live, how will I pay the bills, and will I be alone for the rest of my life? These fears are somewhat irrational, because no one knows the future. To avoid being paralyzed by uncertainty, recognize that you can't know what will happen next, whether you get a divorce or stay married.

Fear of Being Poor

Most people worry about not having enough money to pay their bills after a divorce. The solution is to focus on the assets and income you currently own and develop a budget for your post-divorce life. Calculate the value of the community assets you own, and then decide which ones you want to keep post-divorce. You will likely want the brokerage account rather than the pension, because you will need cash to pay bills after a divorce, and retirement accounts incur penalties for early withdrawals. If you already have a job, that's great. If not, start looking for one so you can support yourself. Once you know the approximate value of your assets and monthly income, you can develop a post-divorce budget and begin to master your fear of being poor. With a little advance planning, you will be fine.

Fear of Being Alone

The fear of being alone is caused by our need to avoid abandonment. As children, we had a caretaker who generally kept us safe and secure. It's reasonable to be dependent when you're three, but as an adult, you need to take care of yourself. If you fear being abandoned, you may have transferred your childhood dependency to your spouse and become so anxious about abandonment that it's paralyzing you. Being lonely is a fact of life—you can feel alone in a marriage as well as after a divorce. The answer is to take responsibility for your own happiness and not remain dependent on others.

Fear for Your Children

Divorce is stressful for kids. However, they generally recover and are fine in a year or two, especially if you are able to continue being a loving parent. In fact, children in high-conflict families are better off after divorce, because their parents aren't fighting all the time. Children are adaptable, so divorce has few lasting consequences for the majority of them. To minimize problems, parents should avoid fighting in front of the kids, maintain a loving relationship with their children, and help them understand their feelings about the divorce.

Fear of Emotional Pain

Divorce causes grief, shock, depression, fear, and anger. These negative feelings are common in everyone who suffers a serious loss and are a natural reaction to divorce. The first feelings are usually shock and denial. As denial disappears, we often mask our grief with anger. Next come thoughts of what we can do to prevent the divorce. Following the bargaining stage, many people become depressed or angry again. After about a year, the sense of loss diminishes, and most people come to terms with their grief and pain. Loss is an inevitable part of life. Grieving is a personal process, and there is no "right" way to handle it—but you must experience the pain to recover from your divorce.

Change is stressful, and getting a divorce can be frightening. However, starting a new life can be liberating if you become more independent and self-sufficient. The key to surviving a divorce is to face your fears and learn to cope with life's challenges on your own. The more you know about divorce, finances, and mental health, the better you can handle the emotional pain of a divorce. If you are afraid you can't support yourself, develop a budget and find a way to make money. If you are worried about your kids, see a psychologist and discuss what you can do to help them cope with the divorce. If you are overwhelmed because you don't know what to expect from a divorce, read this book and meet with a collaborative attorney to learn about the divorce process. Knowledge will help you face your fears and overcome them.

How to Tell the Kids about Divorce

A Detailed Guide to Telling Your Children You Are Getting a Divorce

Telling the children about divorce is one of the most difficult conversations parents ever have. Most children want their parents to stop fighting and stay together, so telling them Mommy and Daddy are going to divorce is tough for everyone. Children remember the "divorce talk" all their lives. There is no perfect way to break the news, but below are a few tips about how to proceed that can minimize the stress and damage.

Agree on a Message

Talk to your spouse ahead of time and develop a simple message that explains what's happening. Make certain you are going to divorce before you talk to the children. Don't blame each other. Deliver the speech calmly. Use "we" in discussing the divorce, and avoid bitterness. Keep the message simple and neutral.

Include the Whole Family

If possible, both of you need to talk to all your children at the same time and answer each child's concerns. Pick a quiet time when nothing is happening—a weekend is best. Expect additional questions later.

Write a Script

This is such an important conversation; you need to get it right, so plan the major points you want to make and outline them. Tell your children you love them, that the divorce is not their fault, both Mommy and Daddy will still be in their lives, and you will minimize disruption as much as possible.

Expect Different Reactions

Children will react differently. Some may be relieved that the fighting may stop, while others may be frightened or angry that things are going to change. Younger children will generally be egocentric, while older children are able to understand more about the divorce. Children need routines, so make only essential changes. Be honest about how the divorce is going to affect them, and stick to your promises.

Alert Teachers and Friends

Tell their teachers, doctors, and friends' parents about the divorce, so they will be prepared. Say you want them to be sensitive and supportive of your children, but request that they don't ask your children about the divorce.

Tell Children What's Going to Happen

Tell the children about your plan for the divorce, where Daddy is going to live, whether the children have to move, about their friends, and anything else they ask about. Try to make them comfortable, and address their concerns honestly.

Allow Children to Discuss Feelings

Don't be surprised by any reaction you get. Some children will be angry, others relaxed. Some will be sad and others quiet.

Invite them to discuss their feelings when they have processed the news.

Assure Them It Will Work Out

Explain to your children that change is difficult and it takes time to adjust. Assure them of your love and protection. Most of all, try to interact with your spouse as an adult, because your children will be watching and wondering if you will still take care of them. Let them see you as competent adults, not squabbling children.

Ask for Help

If you are feeling overwhelmed, or if your children seem depressed, are acting out, or their grades drop, seek professional help. You may want to find a counselor who can talk with you and your children, together or individually.

Consider the Age of Each Child

Up to five years of age, children are totally dependent on their parents and have little ability to understand what will happen in the future. For young children, telling them you are divorcing and you love them should be sufficient. Look for signs of fear, anger, regression, or emotional instability. Between six and ten years of age, children become able to think; they can understand the future and discuss their feelings. However, they still have limited abilities to understand a divorce. They often see events in black and white and may blame one parent. They need to understand that the decision to divorce was not their fault. Older children have more capacity to understand a divorce. They will want to be more independent and develop relationships outside the family. Try to maintain regular routines and disrupt their lives as little as possible.

Three things help children survive the trauma of divorce: maintaining a strong relationship with both parents, receiving adequate parenting during and after the divorce, and minimizing exposure to family conflict. Losing a father or mother can happen if one parent drifts away or is undermined by the other parent, and that's not constructive. Maintain good parenting skills by taking a parenting class every year or so. Avoiding conflict is best done by entering the collaborative divorce process and avoiding litigation.

Dealing with a Narcissist

How to Handle a Narcissistic Spouse during a Divorce

A narcissist has little understanding of people and no ability to empathize with others. He or she feels flawed, inadequate, and ashamed. The narcissist is critical, self-centered, and manipulative. He or she craves attention, needs to be in control, and seeks status, money, power, and recognition. Narcissists need to protect their fragile egos by being defensive and intimidating others. During a collaborative divorce, a narcissist may appear normal except when subjected to stress. In a litigated divorce, the narcissist may appear defensive and withdrawn or angry and hostile.

Signs of Narcissism

A narcissist accepts no responsibility for difficulties, becomes enraged when criticized, denies he or she has problems, cannot admit to a mistake, feels he or she needs to be perfect, is critical of others, and becomes passive-aggressive when angry. A major problem with a narcissist during a collaborative divorce is that he or she ignores boundaries by making others feel guilty, devalued, and intimidated. The narcissist creates self-doubt about others' perception of reality.

Dealing with a Narcissist

There are several steps you can take to handle a narcissistic spouse during a collaborative divorce. First, you need to maintain your own self-confidence. Feeling secure about your own worth will allow you to remain calm in the middle of an argument and avoid getting angry. Ask for a time-out when your narcissistic spouse becomes enraged, and give him or her time to calm down. Don't argue, because it won't do any good, and you will just become frustrated. Trying to get the narcissist to listen to reason is a waste of time because he or she doesn't want to hear what you have to say. Your narcissistic spouse needs to protect his or her fragile ego by attacking you, putting you down, and denying reality. Try to remain calm, and allow the collaborative process to work.

Narcissists Feel above the Law

Normal people are able to give and take during collaborative divorce interactions, but a narcissist feels his or her needs are most important and special; he or she has difficulty understanding how this behavior affects others and finds it difficult to compromise. Narcissists believe rules don't apply to them. Consequently, they often say or do things during a collaborative divorce that are misleading or produce resentment or anger. Narcissists are unaware they have social and emotional problems, don't know they are lying, and blame others for their problems. A narcissist believes he or she is a victim. The major problems with narcissists are that they have little empathy and believe their needs are most important.

Collect Financial Documents Early

Narcissists need to control others, and one way they do that is by withholding financial documents. To avoid this problem during a collaborative divorce, begin collecting financial documents from other sources as soon as possible. Go to your bank and broker to collect records; make copies of all financial documents in the house before you announce you want a divorce; run a credit check on yourself and your spouse; get copies of your tax records from the IRS.

Don't Accept Blame

Don't allow a narcissist to make you feel guilty or intimidated. Don't allow yourself to become a victim. Most of all, don't be fooled by your spouse's claim that the divorce is all your fault—difficult relationships are usually caused by both parties. Protect your interests during the collaborative divorce, and don't trust him or her to tell the truth. Verify all documents, make certain he or she isn't hiding anything, and get everything in writing. Don't attack a narcissist—he or she will just become defensive and difficult.

A Narcissist May Seek Revenge

Many narcissists never get over being rejected. They will blame their spouses and may seek revenge after the divorce. A drawn-out divorce can be emotionally and financially draining. To avoid these problems, opt for a collaborative divorce, try to negotiate a fair settlement, arrange custody exchanges in a public place, never argue with your ex-spouse in front of the children, and engage a counselor to help you cope with your own feelings. One way to protect yourself post-divorce is to avoid personal contact with your narcissistic ex-spouse as much as possible; when you must meet personally, keep it to a minimum. Use the phone or e-mail rather than meeting in person. Consider the possibility of parental alienation, (where one parent says bad things about the other parent and attempts to alienate the children from him or her) and take it seriously if you see signs that it's happening. Also, ask for a parenting coordinator during negotiations to help you and your ex-spouse deal with co-parenting issues after the divorce is final.

No matter how you choose to divorce, dealing with a narcissistic spouse can be difficult. However, it's better to avoid litigation if possible by entering into a collaborative divorce. Explain to your narcissistic spouse that he or she will save money, have privacy, and be better able to control the outcome. These benefits will appeal to his or her needs.

Managing Emotions during Divorce

A Psychological Guide to Handling Your Emotions during the Divorce

Getting through a divorce will be less stressful if you approach it as the termination of a business partnership rather than seeing it as personal rejection. That's hard, because divorce generates strong feelings that can complicate the process. Anger and grief are natural reactions to loss and may interfere with resolving your dispute. In the middle of a divorce, ordinary anger and sadness can morph into rage or depression if you're not careful. Strong emotions make a divorce more costly and divisive. Maintaining a rational attitude will make divorce less stressful and expensive for both of you.

Divorce as Termination of a Partnership

Your divorce will be less stressful and costly if you think of your marriage as a business partnership and recognize that the goal of divorce is a dissolution agreement that meets the important interests of both spouses. If you both approach divorce with a rational attitude, you can avoid being overwhelmed by anger and grief. Moreover, selecting a collaborative divorce that gives clients better control over the outcome will help you stay involved, feel you are making progress, and leave you both better off financially and emotionally.

What Options Are Available?

There are two basic ways to divorce in Texas: collaborative or litigation. A collaborative divorce allows clients to negotiate outside the courthouse and encourages a rational approach to the divorce process. In contrast, litigation generates additional stress and anger and can prolong the divorce. In a collaborative divorce, the couple gathers around a conference table with two attorneys, a neutral mental-health professional, and a neutral financial professional to resolve their dispute. This collaborative team guides them through the process with less strife, emotional damage, and bitterness. It's a divorce with dignity. If the collaborative process reaches an impasse, the attorneys may recommend collaborative mediation to overcome the impasse, or they must resign, and the clients have to engage new litigation attorneys. About 96 percent of collaborative divorce cases resolve without going to court. In a traditional litigation divorce, the attorneys fight over discovery, hold hearings to resolve disagreements, and settle the case at the last minute or try it before a judge or jury. Litigation is more stressful, expensive, and destructive of family relations than a collaborative divorce. Court battles often make it difficult for the couple to co-parent after the breakup. The one major advantage of litigation is that you can force a spouse who won't compromise to settle, or the court will do it for him or her.

Being Proactive Minimizes Stress

The collaborative divorce process causes less stress because it's organized and proactive. The parties, their attorneys, and the neutral professionals jointly collect financial documents, evaluate assets and liabilities, and characterize property as community or separate. Marital property is preserved and stressful emotions minimized because the parties don't fight about ambiguous financial information or discovery disputes. Having available all financial documents necessary to prove the character and value of assets and liabilities avoids disagreements and speeds resolution of the dispute.

Anger and Grief

Anger and grief are natural responses to divorce because your entire life is turned upside down. You may feel your spouse is rejecting you, threatening to take your children, and wanting all your money. Loss causes hurt, pain, grief, and anger. However, strong emotions will interfere with a rational approach to divorce. If your anger or grief gets out of control and begins to dominate your life, seek professional help. It's natural to feel hurt from the loss of love, and it's unpleasant to feel the pain of rejection. Don't allow your anger to control you, and don't use it as a shield to avoid experiencing your pain and grief. If you don't control your anger and experience the pain, your divorce will take longer and you will need more time to heal. Use your anger as motivation to work through your loss maturely, resolve your divorce rationally, and move on to develop a new life for yourself.

Don't be afraid of your feelings during a divorce, but don't let them get out of control. Anger and grief can sabotage a rational approach to divorce. Try to think about marriage as a partnership and divorce as the dissolution of a business. It's difficult to manage your feelings during litigation because going to court is stressful, expensive, and destructive of family relations. Collaborative divorce minimizes stress and will help you maintain a balanced, rational approach to divorce. Try to control your feelings and approach your divorce calmly—it will lower the stress, speed the process, and minimize the cost.

Surviving Divorce Financially

How to Protect Yourself Financially during a Divorce

Divorce can be financially debilitating, no matter how long you've been married. It's especially difficult when it comes late in life. The emotional pain is greater because you have so many shared memories, and the financial pain is often worse because you have less time to recoup the loss before retirement. The grim reality is that 25 percent of divorces happen after fifty years of age, so older couples need to plan ahead to survive a gray divorce. Even if you are younger, you need to plan financially to make it through the divorce. Here are seven tips to help you.

Get Advice

Whether you litigate or choose a collaborative divorce, you need expert guidance. If you decide on a collaborative divorce, your attorney, a neutral financial professional, and a neutral mental-health professional are available to guide you through the process. If you decide to litigate your divorce, you should engage or meet with a financial professional to help you organize and understand your financial situation.

Develop a Budget

Once you have your advisors on board, work out a post-divorce budget that is realistic and ensures a comfortable lifestyle for you, given the more limited resources you will have post-divorce. Two households are more expensive than one, and the money you receive from the divorce settlement may not be adequate for the lifestyle you enjoyed in the past. You may have to cut corners to guarantee enough funding for retirement, and you may have to work longer to make up the difference.

Understand Your Finances

Collect a complete list of all your assets, including your home, vehicles, personal property, saving accounts, checking accounts, brokerage accounts, pensions, health benefits, annuities, life insurance, social security, and any other assets you own. Divide the assets into those that are your separate property (assets you owned prior to marriage or acquired by gift or inheritance), and understand that the remainder of your assets are community property and will be divided roughly equally between you and your spouse during the divorce. Make certain you understand the tax consequences of various assets—for example, funds in an IRA are not equal to dollars in a savings account, because IRA funds will be taxed when withdrawn and will incur a penalty if withdrawn early.

Plan Where to Live

Decide whether you want to keep the family home, sell it to your spouse, or put it on the market and divide the proceeds. Before you choose to keep the family home, make certain you understand the costs involved, including paying your spouse for half the equity in the home; paying the mortgage, taxes, utilities, maintenance, and help with gardening and other chores as you age. It's rarely smart to keep a large house for one person. Think about downsizing to a townhouse or a condominium if you are going to be living alone.

Consider Your Health and Mobility

An unexpected difficulty of gray divorce is that you won't have a spouse to care for you if your health declines or you lose mobility as you age. You will need to plan for current health costs and long-term assisted-living facilities when you can't continue to live alone.

Stay in Touch with Family

If you have adult children, stay in touch with them and your grandchildren, if you are blessed with some. They can be a source of comfort, entertainment, and social support. Don't put them in the middle of your divorce, because they will resent it and may not want to see either of you after the divorce is finished.

See a Counselor

Divorce at any age is emotionally difficult, but as you grow older and become more set in your ways, it's especially difficult to face the changes you will endure during and after a divorce. If you feel anxious, depressed, or alone, you should see a psychologist who can help you handle the grief caused by divorce.

Once you have assembled a collaborative team, collected your financial records, developed a budget, gained an understanding of your assets, planned your living arrangements, considered your health and mobility needs, made arrangements to stay in contact with your family, and seen a psychologist to deal with the anxiety and grief associated with a divorce, you are not finished. Once your divorce if final, you need a post-divorce estate plan. The Texas Estate and Family Code will keep your former spouse from inheriting your assets, but you need a new estate plan to ensure your assets are inherited by the proper beneficiaries. You need a new a will, power of attorney, medical power of attorney, directive to physicians, and HIPAA release. If you have substantial assets, you may want to consider a trust or family limited partnership to protect assets from creditors and reduce or eliminate estate taxes.

Divorce Negotiation

A Detailed Guide to Negotiation and Compromise during a Collaborative Divorce

In a collaborative divorce, couples negotiate and compromise to reach a fair settlement of their dispute. However, many people don't know how to negotiate or compromise effectively. It's not difficult to learn; both negotiation and compromise are based on either power or trust. Using power during negotiation often creates an impasse, so I don't recommend it as the best approach to settlement. Instead, I suggest you and your attorney work at developing trust with your spouse and use interest-based negotiation to settle your divorce dispute in a collaborative manner.

Adversarial Negotiation

The goal in adversarial bargaining is to win. Each party wants more of everything, and they don't care about the other side's needs. Adversarial negotiation is based on power, and each side attempts to undermine the other's confidence, in order to negotiate a better outcome for themselves. Adversarial negotiation involves taking positions and sticking to them while trying to intimidate the other side. Adversarial bargaining often produces an impasse because neither side trusts the other, and they often refuse to compromise. Needless to say, adversarial bargaining rarely leads to a satisfactory settlement because they find it difficult to compromise. Adversarial divorces often end up before a judge or jury rather than getting settled.

Cooperative Negotiation

This style of negotiation is the opposite of adversarial bargaining because collaborative negotiators seek a settlement that meets both parties' goals and interests. For example, an interest-based goal involving the house might be to keep the children in the same school district so they can see their friends. This goal can be met by awarding the family home to the custodial parent, selling the family home and renting a smaller home in the same area, or trading for a smaller house in the same school district. The collaborative process works better if the parties are able to trust each other, but trust may be in short supply during a difficult divorce. There are various ways to develop trust between parties if they want to use collaborative bargaining and learn to compromise.

Building Trust

Trust is the foundation of cooperative bargaining. Parties who trust each other share information, communicate honestly, and engage in good-faith negotiation. There are several ways to develop and maintain trust during negotiation. First, the parties should make eye contact and listen actively. Active listening involves acknowledging the other party's feelings, listening with an open mind, and respecting the other party's positions. It helps if both parties can stay calm in the face of strong emotions and allow the other person to express his or her feelings without becoming defensive. Also, expressing honest appreciation for the other party's efforts to compromise can build trust. Interest-based negotiators see the other party as a problem-solving partner rather than an adversary. They understand each party has different priorities, and they try to meet everyone's goals while reaching a fair settlement. Interest-based negotiators maintain cooperation by being courteous and by ensuring that the negotiation is fair.

How to Compromise

Negotiators must make concessions to settle their case, otherwise they will reach an impasse. Cooperative negotiators generally begin with a realistic opening offer and adjust the size and speed of their concessions to match offers from the other side. Smart negotiators make smaller concessions as they approach agreement. However, offering a small concession after the other side makes a generous offer can damage trust and generate anger. If the other side makes a large concession, follow with one of similar size to encourage progress. On the other hand, if the other side makes small concessions, move in similar small steps toward settlement. Try signaling that you are willing to make larger concessions if they will reciprocate, but don't give away the store.

Never make a large concession near the end of settlement discussions, because the other side will believe you are eager to settle and may become entrenched in their current position. Interest-based negotiators often split the difference at the very end of bargaining to seal the deal. Psychologically, this makes everyone feel they got a fair deal.

Zone of Agreement

An important goal of interest-based negotiation is to discover a zone of agreement that meets the important goals and interests of both sides. The parties can't reach an agreement unless they find acceptable options that meet the major needs of both. If there are no acceptable options within the zone of agreement, the parties must change their evaluation of existing options or generate new ones until they discover a settlement option within the agreement zone.

Don't Mislead During Negotiations

Collaborative attorneys don't misrepresent facts during negotiation, because that will damage trust and make negotiation more difficult or even impossible. Some psychologically sensitive professionals believe they can tell if someone is lying by observing their body language and speech patterns. These professionals pay attention to pauses in speech, stutters, or false starts because they believe these behaviors are signs of stress and may indicate lying. In addition, these same professionals pay attention to a voice pitched higher than usual, shifts in posture, and words that are inconsistent with body language (for example, saying no and nodding yes) as signs of stress and possible lying.

Cooperative negotiation is a powerful way to generate creative settlements. Because negotiating a divorce settlement is primarily an emotional experience, it's essential to understand the psychology of negotiation, learn how to develop trust, be able to compromise, and understand your own feelings during the negotiation process.

Child Custody in Texas

A Summary of Texas Law about Child Custody

"Before you decide where you'd like to live, look who's setting up shop in my living room."

The parenting plan governs child custody and determines who may exercise various parental rights and duties, who pays child support, and whether a parenting coordinator is needed to facilitate co-parenting after the divorce. Developing a parenting plan can be difficult for couples who are angry or in the middle of litigation, but in a collaborative divorce, the attorneys and mental-health professional help both parties develop an effective parenting plan that meets the needs of their children.

Joint or Sole Managing Conservatorship?

In a joint managing conservatorship, the parenting plan states which decisions parents make together, which decisions they may make independently, and which decisions only one parent can make. Joint managing conservatorship is preferred in Texas if it's in the children's best interest. If sole managing conservatorship is ordered because the court believes that's in the children's best interest, the sole managing parent is given the right to make all major decisions, select where the children live, and receive child support.

Rights of a Sole Managing Conservator

A sole managing conservator has the exclusive right to decide where the children live, he or she can consent to invasive medical or dental procedures, psychiatric or psychological treatment of the children, and decide about the children's education. He or she can also consent to marriage or enlistment in the armed forces, represent the child in legal actions, and receive child support. Both the sole managing and possessory conservators have the right to receive information about their children's health, education, and welfare and may confer with the other parent before making decisions. Both parents have a right to access medical, dental, educational, and psychological records and attend school activities. They can also be designated as an emergency contact and consent to emergency medical treatment.

Rights and Duties of Joint Managing Conservators

In a joint managing conservatorship, some parental rights and duties are exclusive to one parent, others are shared between the parents, and a few are exercised jointly with the consent of the other parent. The allocation of rights and duties is based on the best interest of the children and is designed to minimize disruptions in their lives. An exclusive right or duty means that only one parent may exercise the right or carry out the duty. The parent who enjoys the exclusive right may act without the other parent's agreement or consent. An independent right is one that each parent can exercise alone, but it may require notice or consultation with the other parent. A joint right may be exercised only with the agreement of the other parent. In this case, each parent has a veto over the action. The parenting plan must designate one parent to have the exclusive right to determine the children's residence and receive child support.

When Does a Court Order Joint Custody?

Joint custody is preferred in Texas because it's public policy to encourage both parents to stay involved with their children. Only in cases where there's a problem with one parent will the court award sole custody to the other parent. Generally, children benefit from having contact with both parents.

Why Does a Court Order Sole Custody?

There are three major reasons courts order sole custody: one parent does not want the responsibility of being an involved parent; there's a history of family violence, substance abuse, criminality, or parental abandonment; and in cases where the parents can't agree about education, medical, and religious values.

What's the Difference Between Custody and Possession?

In Texas, custody concerns the rights and duties of the parents, while possession governs physical access to the child. Unless a parent is dangerous to the physical or emotional well-being of the children, courts allow both parents access to their children, although sometimes a parent needs supervision, because of alleged substance abuse, for example. Usually, one parent has primary possession of the children while the other parent will have visitation rights. Standard visitation includes possessing the children on the first, third, and fifth weekends of each month, having dinner with the children in the middle of the week, visits during holidays, and an extended possession period during the summer.

Can a Child Decide Where He or She Wants to Live?

If a child in Texas is over twelve years of age, he or she can state a preference, but it's only one factor a court or the parents will use in determining custody arrangements.

What Is Supervised Visitation?

A court may order supervised visitation if the judge believes it's in the children's best interest and there is clear evidence that the supervised parent may pose a threat to the physical or emotional well-being of the children.

Can One Parent Move the Children?

Because it's important to maintain a stable environment for children and close contact with both parents, courts generally discourage moving children away from the other parent. Usually the parties agree or are ordered to keep the children in contiguous counties near both parents until the children become adults. The court may allow a parent to move his or her children for a clear and compelling reason, such as family help or a promising job opportunity, but the parent who moves is primarily responsible for transporting the children to the other parent for visits.

The goal of a parenting plan is to minimize children's exposure to parental conflict by allocating parental rights and duties in a way that allows parents to make constructive decisions for their children. Sometimes, this means one parent makes most of the decisions, while in other plans, the parents share most rights and duties.

Standard Possession in Texas

A Clear Explanation of Child Custody in Texas

Texas courts generally allow one parent to determine where the children will reside and award the other parent access to the children according to a standard possession schedule. However, in a collaborative divorce, parents can agree to other possession times if it's more convenient for them and in the best interest of the children. Texas has two standard possession schedules: one for parents who reside near each other and one for parents who reside more than a hundred miles apart.

Parents Who Reside Near Each Other

Standard possession for a parent who resides less than a hundred miles from the children's residence gives him or her access for two hours every Thursday from 6:00 to 8:00 p.m., or if he or she prefers, overnight until school resumes Friday. In addition, the possessory conservator has access to the children every first, third, and fifth weekend of each month beginning at 6:00 p.m. Friday and ending at 6:00 p.m. Sunday. For a child under three, the father should have frequent, short, regular contact with his infant or toddler. (See parenting plans for infants and toddlers—chapter 29.)

For spring vacation, the possessory parent has access in even-numbered years beginning at 6:00 p.m. on the day the children are dismissed from school, and ending at 6:00 p.m. on the day before school resumes. The managing parent has access to the children for spring vacation in odd-numbed years. The possessory parent has access for thirty days each summer. If notice is given by April 1, the possessory parent may have access no earlier than the day after school is dismissed and ending not later than seven days before school resumes. The thirty days must be taken in no more than two separate periods of at least seven consecutive days beginning and ending at 6:00 p.m. Without notice, the possessory parent has access for thirty days beginning at 6:00 p.m. on July 1 and ending at 6:00 p.m. on July 31.

Parents Who Reside More Than One Hundred Miles Apart

The possessory parent who lives more than one hundred miles from his or her children may choose to see them every first, third, and fifth weekend or only one weekend each month, beginning at 6:00 p.m. on Friday and ending at 6:00 p.m. the day before school resumes. He or she must give notice to the managing conservator fourteen days before the desired weekend to see the children. The possessory parent must make his or her choice of one or three weekends ninety days after he or she moves more than one hundred miles from the children's residence. The possessory parent has access to the children every spring vacation, beginning at 6:00 p.m. on the day the children are dismissed from school, and ending at 6:00 p.m. on the day before school resumes. If notice is given by April 1, the possessory parent has access to the children for forty-two days every summer, beginning no earlier than the day after school is dismissed and ending no later than seven days before school resumes. The forty-two days must be taken in no more than two separate periods of at least seven consecutive days beginning and ending at 6:00 p.m. Without notice, the possessory parent has access for forty-two days beginning at 6:00 p.m. on June 15 and ending at 6:00 p.m. on July 27.

Holiday Periods Unaffected by Distance.

These holiday provisions supersede conflicting weekend or Thursday possessions. The possessory parent has access to the children for Christmas vacation during even-numbered years, beginning at 6:00 p.m. on the day school is dismissed and ending at noon on December 28. The managing parent shall have access to the children for the same period at Christmas during odd-numbered years. The possessory parent has access to the children during Thanksgiving vacation in odd-numbered years, beginning when school is dismissed and ending at 6:00 p.m. on the following Sunday. The managing parent shall have access to the children for Thanksgiving vacation during even-numbered years for the same period. For children's birthdays, the parent not in actual possession of the children shall pick them up at 6:00 p.m. and return them at 8:00 p.m. Fathers shall have access to their children beginning at 6:00 p.m. on the day before Father's Day and ending at 6:00 p.m. on Father's Day. Mothers shall have access to their children beginning at 6:00 p.m. on the day before Mother's Day and ending at 6:00 p.m. on Mother's Day.

Weekend Possession Extended by a Holiday

If a weekend possession coincides with a Monday school holiday during the school year or a federal, state, or local Monday holiday during the summer months, the weekend possession shall be extended through 6:00 p.m. on Monday. If a weekend possession coincides with a Friday school holiday or a federal, state, or local holiday that falls on a Friday during the summer months, the weekend possession period begins at 6:00 p.m. on Thursday.

Parenting Plans for Infants and Toddlers

How to Handle Child Custody for Infants and Children under Three

Young children in two-parent families generally form attachments to both parents. However, parent-child attachment can be weakened through diminished contact or severe conflict during a divorce. Consequently, parenting plans for infants should contain consistent possession times, predictable transitions, and adequate frequency of possession to foster or maintain attachment to the possessory parent. If one parent is the primary caregiver, the other parent should have frequent short intervals of possession, to avoid losing contact with his or her infant. A parenting plan for infants, until they reach about eighteen months, needs to be different from a parenting plan for toddlers up to three years. Infants need consistency and frequent, stable contacts that foster healthy attachment to both parents. Toddlers need routines that offer security and reinforce parental attachments; they want to explore the world, but they need a loving parent available to soothe and comfort their distress when they become frightened.

Rules for Divorced Parents of Infants

Divorced parents must find an effective way to share information, because infants and young children change rapidly as they age. Consider using "Our Family Wizard" or some other electronic calendar to share information and schedules. Also, divorcing parents should minimize fighting around their young child, because infants and toddlers are sensitive to strong negative emotions. Try to keep communications calm and businesslike around the young child. Parents need to moderate their negative emotions when interacting around their young children. It's best to be calm and supportive around your offspring, because that will foster a positive self-concept for the infant.

Parenting Plans for Infants (Birth to Eighteen Months)

Parenting plan "A" is most appropriate when one parent has been the primary caregiver. Parenting plan "B" works best when both parents have been involved in day-to-day caregiving.

Parenting plan "A": This plan gives the nonprimary parent three periods of three to four hours with the infant spaced over the week. One schedule that works effectively is to have the nonprimary parent responsible for the infant every Tuesday and Thursday from 4:00 to 7:00 p.m. and every Saturday from 10:00 a.m. to 2:00 p.m.

Parenting plan "B": This plan works when both parents have been extensively involved in caregiving before the divorce. The nonprimary parent is responsible for the infant during two three-to-five-hour intervals and one eight-hour interval spaced throughout the week. A good workable plan is to have the non-primary parent responsible for the infant on Monday and Wednesday from 3:00 to 7:00 p.m. and every Friday beginning at 6:00 p.m. until Saturday at 8:00 a.m.

Parenting Plan for Toddlers (Eighteen Months to Three Years)

Parenting plan "A" is most appropriate when one parent has been the primary caregiver before the divorce. Parenting plan "B" works best when both parents have been extensively involved in day-to-day caregiving for their toddler.

Parenting plan "A": Under this plan, the nonprimary parent enjoys three longer periods of interaction with and responsibility for the toddler, spaced evenly throughout the week. One schedule that works effectively is to have the nonprimary parent care for the toddler every Tuesday and Thursday from 3:00 p.m. to 7:00 p.m. and every Saturday from 10:00 a.m. to 4:00 p.m.

Parenting plan "B": This plan works when both parents have been extensively involved in caregiving of their toddler. The nonprimary parent has the toddler for one daytime interval of six hours and two nonconsecutive overnights each week. The toddler should *not* be separated from either parent for more than four days, because infants or toddlers may lose parental attachment if apart from either parent for long intervals.

After three years, most young children can adapt to a standard possession order where the nonprimary parent has the child on the first, third, and fifth weekends of each month, Thursday for dinner each week, alternating intervals during holidays, and for a month during the summer. Gradually shifting from the toddler plan to a standard visitation plan over a month or two works better than an abrupt change. Older children can adapt to other parenting plans, such as shared custody.

Infant and toddler parenting plans are designed to foster attachment to both parents, while maintaining the comfort and security of the offspring. Infants need frequent and consistent contact to develop a strong attachment to both parents. Toddlers need an available loving adult to comfort them and a predictable routine that fosters security. Signs that the parenting plan is not working for an infant include excessive crying, feeding or sleeping problems, withdrawal, irritability, or depression. Signs of distress for toddlers include withdrawal, clinging for more than twenty minutes, changes in eating and toilet habits, and developmental delays. If any of these signs occur, see a professional immediately.

Spousal Maintenance and Alimony

A Discussion of Texas Law about Spousal Support and Contractual Alimony

There are two types of support payments available in Texas: spousal maintenance and contractual alimony. Spousal maintenance is authorized by the Texas Family Code and may be court ordered if the parties meet certain legal criteria. In contrast, contractual alimony is based on IRS rules and an agreement between the parties. Spousal maintenance payments are strictly limited in amount and duration, while contractual alimony payments can be for any amount and length of time, depending on the couple's settlement agreement.

Eligibility for Spousal Maintenance

In Texas, eligibility for spousal maintenance is governed by statute. Maintenance will usually be awarded in cases of adjudicated family violence within two years of the divorce, disability of a spouse or child of the marriage, and for marriages of more than ten years when the spouse has no job skills or work history. Spousal maintenance is intended to support a former spouse while he or she finishes an education or acquires necessary work skills. The most likely way to qualify for spousal maintenance in Texas is to be married more than ten years, lack the ability to support yourself, and have little higher education or few work skills. Most individuals who qualify for spousal maintenance are stay-at-home moms who haven't worked for years. However, a stay-at-home mom will forfeit her right to spousal maintenance if she doesn't actively seek employment or pursue educational opportunities during the divorce.

Limits on Spousal Maintenance

When maintenance is based on disability, the payments may continue as long as the spouse or child of the marriage is disabled. Maintenance based on family violence may last no more than five years. In other cases, the duration of spousal maintenance depends on length of the marriage. If the marriage lasted between ten and twenty years, payments can be for up to five years. If the marriage lasted between twenty and thirty years, payments can be for up to seven years. For marriages over thirty years, spousal maintenance can be ordered for up to ten years. The maximum amount of spousal maintenance that may be ordered by a court is $5,000 per month or 20 percent of the paying spouse's gross monthly income, whichever is less. In setting the amount of maintenance, a court will look at the receiving spouse's "minimum reasonable needs," each spouse's ability to provide for his or her own minimum needs, what assets each spouse will receive from the divorce, and the paying spouse's ability to afford maintenance payments. Maintenance terminates if either party dies or the receiving party cohabits or remarries.

Contractual Alimony.

Contractual alimony may be agreed upon by the spouses and approved by the court. It terminates on the death of either party and may stop if the receiver cohabits or remarries, depending on the agreement. The IRS may disallow a tax deduction if the contractual alimony payments are heavily loaded toward the early years. One advantage of contractual alimony is that the spouse with a higher earning capacity can deduct the payments from his or her income for tax purposes. The receiving spouse will pay tax on the alimony income but at a lower rate. The duration and amount of contractual alimony are set by agreement of the spouses.

The advantages of spousal maintenance are that it can be court ordered and enforced by contempt if a spouse refuses to pay. The disadvantages of spousal maintenance include strict eligibility requirements and limits on the amount and duration of payments. There are several advantages to contractual alimony if the parties can agree on terms, because payments can be tailored to meet specific family needs. For example, if a husband earns a high income and wants to support his children's private education, he can specify that the alimony payments be sent directly to the school while the children are enrolled. If the wife wants to stay in the family home with the children but can't afford the mortgage payments, the husband may agree to pay her contractual alimony, as long as she stays in the home with his children. This way, he is able to keep his children in the family home and close to him so he can maintain his parental relationship.

Child Support in Texas

A Guide to Understanding How Child Support Works in Texas

Child support can be a contentious issue between divorcing parents because the receiving parent can use child support funds however he or she wants, though they are intended for the support of the children. Also, the payments continue until the last child is eighteen or graduates from high school, so the financial stakes can be high. Only a parent can be ordered to pay child support, and most judges follow guidelines established by the Texas legislature, because they are presumed to be reasonable and in the child's best interest.

Guideline Child Support

Child support in Texas is calculated by subtracting the payer's expenses from his or her gross income to generate net monthly income. Gross income includes all income received by the paying spouse. Expense deductions are allowed for taxes, union dues, and health insurance. Net resources are generally capped at $8,550 per month. Child-support payments are calculated by multiplying net monthly resources by percentages based on the number of children involved: 1 = 20 percent; 2 = 25 percent, 3 = 30 percent; 4 = 35 percent, 5 = 40 percent; and for more than five children, not less than 40 percent of net resources. These percentages are reduced if the spouse of children from a prior marriage is also being paid child support by the same spouse.

Above-Guideline Support

The court may order child support payments above guideline or the $8,550 cap if the extra support is justified by the income of the parties and the needs of the children. Examples of reasonable extra needs determined by Texas courts include private-school tuition, a bodyguard, a nanny, travel, music lessons, Christmas presents, and vacations. The court may also determine above-guideline support is just and appropriate if the child has special medical needs, the parents' incomes are high, extra child care is required, or the child has special educational requirements.

Retroactive Child Support.

A parent may be ordered to pay retroactive child support if no support was requested earlier for any reason. The court must apply Texas guidelines to the paying parent's income at the relevant rate for the time when the court is ordering retroactive support. Requests for retroactive child support may be filed up to four years after the child's eighteenth birthday.

Modifying Child Support

Child support may be changed only by a court, although the parties can bring an agreed order to the court for review and signature. Any modification of child support must be in the child's best interest, result from a material and substantial change of circumstances, or be brought three years after the original child-support order was entered.

Enforcement of Child Support

Child-support payments may be enforced by a private attorney or the Texas attorney general's office. A court may order withholding from income, levy against financial assets, and suspend any licenses issued by the state to the delinquent payer. In egregious cases, the court may hold the delinquent payer in contempt and put him or her in jail.

Access and Child Support Are Independent

Possession and access to children can't be withheld simply because the other parent is late paying child support. These are independent rights and duties, and the custodial parent cannot deny the other parent access to the children because he or she is late in paying child support.

The best way to avoid child-support problems is to choose a collaborative divorce. During a collaborative divorce, the parties generally agree on the amount of support that's appropriate, because they know their children's needs and family resources. In a litigated divorce, there is often a dispute about whether child support should be at or above guidelines and may require a hearing before the court.

Tips for Dividing Personal Property

Hints for Dividing Pots, Pans, Jewelry, and Other Personal Property during a Divorce

Personal property consists of all assets except real estate. It includes tangible personal property such as cars, furniture, jewelry, clothing, and intangible personal property such as cash, stocks, bonds, and other financial interests. In a divorce, it's fairly easy to divide intangible financial assets because they have a definite value and can be split according to an agreed percentage. But how do you divide tangible personal property such as pots, pans, and jewelry? The first step is to make a list of all personal items and try to divide them by agreement. If you can't agree on who gets an asset, put it in the "can't divide pool" and follow these tips.

Valuing Personal Property

Minor items such as pots, pans, or toasters aren't worth valuing, because the appraisal cost often exceeds their worth. If you must value an item, try to agree about its worth or check what it sells for on Craigslist. For valuable personal property such as jewelry, coin collections, artwork, or antiques, it may make sense to have these items valued by a professional appraiser.

What about Vehicles?

Here are two approaches for dealing with cars. Most couples agree to "keep our own car" if they are of similar value, because that's an easy solution. If one car is more valuable than the other, go to Kelly Blue Book and get a value for each car based on the same criteria, such as trade-in value to a dealer in good condition. Once you establish values for the vehicles, the person with the more valuable car transfers half the difference in cash or other assets to the other spouse.

How to Divide Jewelry

Generally, jewelry belongs to the person who received it as a gift. It's that individual's separate property, and it doesn't get divided during a divorce. For example, the wife's engagement ring is considered a gift and so it's her separate property. Sometimes, couples make an agreement at the time of marriage or later to return gifted jewelry in the event of a divorce. If a piece of jewelry is a family heirloom, such as grandmother's wedding ring, it should be returned to the spouse whose family originally owned the item. Another approach is to sell the jewelry and divide the cash. However, this may not be a wise financial approach because jewelry doesn't hold its monetary value.

What about Photos and Kids' Art?

Sentimental personal property such as family photos, children's paintings, and baby clothes are usually divided equally between the spouses or given to the spouse who really wants it. In the case of photos, it's possible to digitize them so each spouse can have a complete set. If the spouses can't agree, set those items aside and follow the division tips at the end of this chapter.

Wedding Gifts

Generally, the rule about wedding gifts is that the spouse whose family or friends gave the wedding gift receives it during a divorce. However, there are other methods of dividing wedding gifts, such as awarding the item to the person who used it most of the time during the marriage. For example, it may make sense for the husband to take the drill and sander, while the wife keeps the mixer and toaster.

If you have tried all the above methods and still have personal property that's not divided, use one of the following tried-and-true tricks to divide the remaining personal assets. Flip a coin and allow the winner to select the first item from the remaining pool of personal property. Then let the other spouse select an item and alternate selections until all items are divided. Another approach is to flip a coin for each item, and the person who calls the coin correctly gets that item. A third approach to dividing personal property is to offer to buy an item for say $250. If the other spouse refuses, you can flip the offer and say, "Okay, you can have it for $250." Often, the other spouse will say, "No, I don't want the table. You can have it for $250."

Finally, pets are living creatures, and their best interest should be considered when deciding who will keep them. If both parties want a pet, it sometimes helps to buy another similar pet and flip coins to see who keeps the original pet and who gets the new one.

Dividing Property in Texas

A Discussion of How Community Assets Are Divided under Texas Law

It makes a big difference whether property you own is characterized as separate or community, because you keep all your separate property, while you must divide community property with your spouse in a just and right manner when you divorce. There are several stringent requirements that must be met to prove assets you own are your separate property.

What Is Separate Property?

Property is characterized as separate if you owned or earned it prior to marriage, acquired it by gift or inheritance during marriage, were compensated for a personal injury, or enjoyed a capital gain on separate property.

What Is Community Property?

In Texas, all property is presumed to be community unless you can prove it's separate by clear and convincing evidence. Examples of community property include all income earned during marriage; property bought by community funds or community debt during marriage; all income and dividends earned on stocks, bonds, or other investments owned during marriage; and interest income or cash dividends earned on separate property during marriage.

How Does Property Become Community or Separate?

The character of property is determined when title is acquired. This means if you acquire title to a house prior to marriage using your own funds to buy it, it's separate property. On the other hand, if you acquire a house during marriage, it's community property, unless you bought it with separate money and the lender looked only to your separate credit to pay the mortgage. Once title is acquired and the asset becomes separate property, you can sell the house and buy another without changing its character—it's still separate property because you used the proceeds from the sale of a separate property asset to buy the new house. You must be able to trace the separate funds at the time of divorce, however. All assets bought on credit during marriage are presumed to be purchased with community credit. You may overcome this presumption by showing the creditor agreed to look only to the separate credit of one spouse.

Can You Transform Property?

There are several ways to change the character of property in Texas. For example, spouses can transform community property into separate property by written agreement during marriage through a postnuptial agreement. You may transform separate to community property by commingling funds. If you put separate funds in a community account, it may become community property, unless you can clearly trace the separate funds into and out of the community account.

What Is a Reimbursement Claim?

If you use separate funds to purchase a house and then use community funds to pay the mortgage or add capital improvements to the house, the community estate has a reimbursement claim on the separate property house. The house belongs to one spouse's separate estate, but the community estate has a reimbursement claim on the property because the mortgage principal was partially paid using community funds or the capital improvements paid for by community funds added value to the house. Reimbursement claims need to be proved, and then the separate estate must pay the claim into the community estate, and the funds are divided between the spouses.

How Do You Keep Property Separate?

To maintain the character of separate property, it needs to be deposited into a separate account. Commingling separate and community property can transform the separate property into community property if the separate property can't be traced into and out of the commingled account.

What about My Trust Fund?

If a trust fund was established by your parents or others, the principal of the trust fund is separate property, while any income from interest or dividends that's earned and distributed by the trust during marriage becomes community property.

Can a Couple Agree to Own No Community Property?

Yes, if you execute a postnuptial agreement that transforms all community property into separate property. This arrangement makes it easier to maintain the character of inherited or gifted separate property, especially if the estate is large.

What about Mineral Interests?

Oil and gas interests have the same character as the surface interests because they are considered a depletion of the land. Both royalty and bonus payments are considered separate property if the surface interest was owned separately. However, rental payments are not separate because they simply maintain an operator's right to drill for oil and gas and are not a direct payment for extraction of minerals.

The basic rule in characterizing property is that all assets acquired during marriage are presumed to be community property unless it can be shown by clear and convincing evidence that it's separate property. This is a fairly high standard of proof, so the owner of separate property must be careful to keep separate assets segregated from community funds or maintain good records to aid in tracing the separate asset. If separate and community funds are commingled, the separate property can become a community asset unless you can trace it by clear and convincing evidence. Couples can agree to transform their community property into separate property by signing a postnuptial agreement.

Unequal Property Division

An Explanation of How You May Receive a Larger Share of the Community Estate

"She got custody of the cave, the wheel, *and* the fire!"

Texas courts must divide marital property in a "just and right" manner. However, that doesn't necessarily mean a fifty-fifty split, because there are several factors courts consider in possibly awarding a larger share of the marital estate to one spouse. Whether a spouse receives a larger share of community property depends on the balance of these factors. Even though Texas awards no-fault divorces, if one spouse commits adultery, family violence, a felony, or abandons the marriage, courts may consider that "fault" and award a larger share of community property to the innocent spouse. Courts may consider any of the following factors in deciding to award one spouse a larger share of the marital estate.

Unequal Earning Capacity

If one spouse is a physician who earns $350,000 annually, while the other is a housewife with no employment history, she will likely receive a larger share of the community estate based on this factor alone.

Fault in the Marriage

Courts may award a larger share of the marital estate to an innocent spouse if he or she is the victim of adultery, abuse, abandonment, or the other spouse has been convicted of a felony. However, some courts give fault a smaller weight in their evaluation of the case compared to earning capacity, age, health, and length of marriage.

Length of Marriage

Most judges are willing to award a larger share of the community estate to a spouse who has been caring for children rather than working full time, especially if the marriage was a long one. Judges believe a stay-at-home mom should be compensated for her nonfinancial contribution to the family estate.

Custody of Minor Children

Courts consider the welfare of children when dividing property, so the spouse who receives primary custody of minor children may be awarded a larger share of the community estate because child support doesn't necessarily cover all the expenses of rearing children.

Fraud or Waste of Community Funds

Courts will punish a spouse who has wasted community assets by spending them on a paramour. If a spouse committed fraud by, for example, hiding community assets, courts may award the innocent spouse a larger share of the marital estate as compensation. Generally, courts calculate the amount of waste or fraud and award 50 percent of that amount to the innocent spouse above and beyond his or her regular community estate entitlement.

Size of Separate Estate

If one spouse inherited a sizeable estate from his or her family, the courts may take that fact into consideration when dividing marital assets and award the other spouse a larger share of community funds.

Health and Age of Spouses

If one spouse is ill, disabled, or significantly older, the courts generally award him or her a larger share of the community estate, based on their inability to continue earning a living.

Education and Abilities of Spouses

The spouse who does not have an advanced professional degree or special abilities, such as being a professional athlete or singer, may be awarded a larger share of the community estate to compensate him or her for the difference in earning capacity.

Need for Future Support

If the marriage lasted less than ten years, so there is no right to spousal support, courts may award a larger share of the marital estate to the spouse who needs support to attend college or vocational training so he or she can gain the skills needed to earn a living.

Courts consider many factors when deciding to award a larger share of the marital property to one spouse, including unequal earning capacity, fault, length of marriage, custody of minor children, fraud, waste, size of a separate estate, health, age, education, and need for future support. Generally, the more important factors are unequal earning capacity, fraud, health, age, and need for future support. The courts balance these factors when making an unequal asset division. For example, if the factors favoring one spouse are balanced with the factors favoring the other, the court will often decide on close to a fifty-fifty division of assets. On the other hand, if several factors favor one spouse, he or she will usually be awarded a larger share of the marital estate, compared with a spouse who has only one or two factors on his or her side.

Collaborative Mediation

An Explanation of How Mediation Can Break an Impasse in a Collaborative Divorce

When a collaborative divorce negotiation reaches an impasse, the parties often decide to take their dispute to collaborative mediation for settlement rather than opt for litigation. Mediation occurs in three stages: competition, cooperation, and problem solving. Clients need to understand these stages, because it's difficult to make progress in a collaborative mediation if one party expects cooperation and the other side is still being competitive. During the early stages of collaborative mediation, it's best to develop trust and manage emotions rather than try to settle issues. Settlement usually happens during the later stages of collaborative mediation.

Who Should Mediate?

Collaborative mediation can succeed with many types of clients, but it works best for couples who share some trust, have realistic expectations, believe they can control the outcome, and don't have a power imbalance. It also helps if clients have effective communication skills and are able to manage their emotions. Effective collaborative mediation candidates are able to put themselves in the other person's shoes and avoid insulting them. In contrast, clients who are dishonest, have mental-health or substance-abuse issues are less suitable for collaborative mediation, although mediation can still work in these more difficult cases.

Keys to Success

The keys to a successful collaborative mediation include understanding the other side's position, establishing trust, correcting power imbalances, being realistic, and knowing when and how to compromise. Both sides need to understand that nothing is agreed until all issues are settled, so there's no misunderstanding. Keeping good records will help later if there is disagreement about what was said or agreed.

Dealing with Bad Faith

A particularly difficult problem occurs in collaborative mediation when one side believes the other party is acting in bad faith. When this happens, it's important for each side to openly discuss their concerns with the mediator and their attorney. If one side believes the other party is not bargaining in good faith, it's difficult to reach agreement because there's a lack of basic trust. The best approach is for the mediator to tell both parties it's counterproductive to attribute bad faith to the other side just because you disagree with them. Strong disagreement doesn't usually mean the other side is acting in bad faith. It may be that the other party simply believes passionately in his or her position. Collaborative mediation will proceed more quickly and successfully if both parties assume the other side is acting in good faith and they can keep an open mind. It's also helpful for both sides to look at the facts from the other party's point of view, because it will help them compromise and reach an agreement.

Don't Try to Recoup Sunk Costs

An impasse can occur if a party does not understand the concept of sunk costs, which are losses that can't be recouped. It makes no sense to throw good money after bad trying to regain assets that are already lost. In a collaborative mediation, it's better to accept a reasonable settlement than to spend more money to litigate the case and run the risk that you may lose both the cost of litigation and the gains that could have been achieved through settlement negotiations. This is particularly relevant when the parties are facing huge litigation costs if they can't settle. Avoiding the cost of litigation can save thousands of dollars, so it's often better to accept a smaller settlement than gamble on getting a larger settlement at trial after paying the huge emotional and financial costs of litigation. There's no guarantee either client will win at trial.

Collaborative mediation can be an effective way to break an impasse when an issue proves too difficult to resolve during joint collaborative negotiations. By involving a neutral third-party mediator who is collaboratively trained and understands how to deal with divorce issues, the collaborative case can be settled and litigation avoided. The key is to engage a sensitive, experienced, well-trained collaborative mediator who is trusted by both parties. He or she can suggest solutions that may have been rejected before. However, because they are now coming from an experienced and trusted neutral, they can be heard by both parties, and the case can be settled.

Helping Children during and after Divorce

Hints for Supporting Your Children during and after the Divorce

Divorce can be a life-changing experience for some children and can cause behavioral problems if not handled properly. Happily, most children return to normal a year or so after the divorce. Children in high-conflict families may be better off following a divorce compared with similar children who remain in high-conflict families with their parents fighting all the time. In contrast, children from low-conflict families fare worse following a divorce compared with similar children whose parents stay married, although they generally recover in a year or so. Divorce may have lasting effects on some vulnerable children. For example, children of divorce are three times more likely to divorce, compared with children from intact families. Two things that help children cope are to maintain peer friendships and parental love during and after the divorce.

Resilient Children

Some children are more adaptable, and divorce causes fewer problems for them. Specifically, children who are friendly and adjust easily to change have less difficulty dealing with divorce, compared with children who are shy and have difficulty handling new arrangements. Children with good social skills, who are friendly and understand others' feelings, adapt more easily to divorce, compared with shy and socially awkward children.

Parenting

The way divorcing parents handle their children makes a significant difference in how they adjust to divorce. For example, if the parents avoid fighting in front of their children; keep the children out of their disputes; and maintain a consistent, loving relationship with their children, divorce has few negative effects on the children. On the other hand, if parents fight in front of the children, put them in the middle of their arguments, and don't give them consistent love at this difficult time, the children suffer and will have a more difficult time adjusting after the divorce.

Emotional Coaching

Some children worry that their parents' divorce was their fault or that their parents don't want them anymore. Other children feel angry, withdrawn, or isolated during the divorce. Feelings of guilt, rejection, anger, or isolation can have lasting negative effects on children. Emotional coaching of children by their parents can help them deal with these strong negative feelings caused by a divorce. Parents can help their children deal with divorce by teaching them to pay attention to their feelings, discussing emotions with the children, listening to the children talk about their feelings, labeling feelings in words children can understand, and helping children deal with emotionally difficult situations.

Maintaining Children's Friendships

Aside from having a resilient child, avoiding fighting in front of the children, not putting them in the middle of disputes, and helping them handle feelings, what else can parents do to cushion the shock of a divorce? One other important factor is to maintain children's friendships with school-age peers. Parents should make every effort to keep their children in the same school during and after the divorce. Staying in the family home is another good idea if financially possible. If not, try to stay in the same neighborhood, so the children can attend their usual school and see their friends. Planning activities with your children's friends may be more difficult after the divorce because there are two parents involved who live in separate houses. If the divorced parents aren't communicating, it's generally more difficult to foster children's friendships. Friendly co-parenting, which happens automatically after a collaborative divorce, will make a strong, positive difference in children's lives.

Divorce causes significant distress for children. Most adapt to divorce after one or two years, but a small minority continue to experience problems. Children in high-conflict families are generally better off following divorce, but some children from low-conflict families do worse after a divorce for a year or so. Children adapt better if they are encouraged to maintain friendships with peers during and after the divorce. Parents should keep children in the same school if possible, so they can see their friends. Make sure your children's friends know how to contact both parents. However, don't be surprised if some of your children's friends' parents become wary after the divorce. They may see you as a threat, or they may be fearful for their own marriage. If some of your children's friends drift away, don't worry. Help them make new ones.

How to Enjoy the Holidays during a Divorce

Advice for Surviving the Holidays When You Are Divorcing

The holidays intensify feelings of loss and loneliness when you are in the middle of a difficult divorce. It can be depressing to be alone at Thanksgiving or Christmas. Don't sit around feeling sorry for yourself. Make plans to be with friends, family, and your children during the holidays. Contact your estranged spouse, and discuss how both of you will deal with the children during the holidays. If the children are old enough, get them involved in the planning. Just because you are in the middle of a divorce doesn't mean you can't plan a fun holiday for the whole family; it's a good way to begin effective co-parenting.

Plan New Holiday Adventures

If being together as a family won't work, plan to have the children over to your house the day before or after a holiday for a second celebration. Don't spend a holiday alone—have lunch with an old friend, go to a play, or do something that makes you happy.

Reassure Your Children

Talk with your children about the holidays and let them know things will be different, but you still love them. Tell the children exactly what is planned for the holidays, and stick to the plan, because any additional change is difficult at this time.

Stay in Touch

Even if you can't be with your children on a holiday, that's no reason you can't communicate with them. Call your children, send a small present, or mail a card with a short message of love and include money with the card. However, don't intrude on their time with your separated spouse—he or she needs time with the children as well.

Focus on Your Children

Focus on your children and others rather than feeling sorry for yourself during the holidays. Divorce is hard on your spouse and children as well. Money is usually tight during a divorce, so spend time with your children instead of buying lavish presents. They will appreciate seeing you more than receiving an expensive gift.

Make an Advent Calendar

An advent calendar makes counting the days until Christmas more fun for your children, because it's packed with small daily prizes. Advent calendars are easy to make, or you can buy them at a local store. To make an advent calendar, take candy- or trinket-filled colored envelopes and tack them to a calendar board so the children can open one every day before Christmas.

Visit a Tree Farm

Start a new holiday tradition by visiting a tree farm to select and cut your very own Christmas tree. Let your children find the right tree for themselves; it won't be perfect, but so what? When you get the tree home, let the children string the lights and decorate it. They will remember the experience forever.

See the Christmas Lights

Many neighborhoods, businesses, and universities decorate with lights during the holiday season. In late December, take the children around your city, looking at the different lights and Christmas decorations. Take pictures and let each child choose his or her favorite. Make a scrapbook of the best ones.

Read a Christmas Story

Find a favorite Christmas story and begin an annual tradition by reading it on Christmas Eve before bedtime. If you can't be with your children on Christmas Eve, record a story and send it to them so they can hear your voice reading to them on that special evening.

Hunt for Presents

Remove the presents from under the tree, and hide them around the house instead. Assemble envelopes from Santa with instructions telling the children where he hid each present. You can give each child an envelope and let them take out slips of paper one at a time and hunt for that present. When they find the present, they can bring it into the living room to open with everyone present.

Bake Cookies with the Kiddies

Stir up some holiday cheer by mixing and baking a batch of fresh cookies with the children. Assign little ones an easy task, such as adding premeasured ingredients to the bowl. Let them roll out the dough and cut or shape it into their favorite cookies. When the cookies are finished and cool, let them eat the fresh cookies with milk.

Holidays can be difficult for you and the children during a divorce. To ease the pain, establish new traditions. If possible, plan a joint Christmas celebration with your spouse, because that will help your children feel you both still love them. If that's impractical, plan new activities for you and your children to enjoy. The important thing is to make certain your children feel loved, especially during this special time of the year.

Can I Date during the Divorce?

Rules of the Road Governing Dating while Divorcing

The question, "Can I date during my divorce?" comes up all the time in my collaborative divorce practice. I tell my clients it's not a good idea because there are too many possible complications. In spite of my advice, clients often date during their divorce. Usually it's because they're lonely and want to feel better about themselves. After all, what could go wrong on a simple date, right? Unfortunately, lots of bad things can happen if you date while your divorce is pending. There are strategic, legal, and emotional reasons not to date during your divorce. If you must date while your divorce is pending, please follow my list of dos and don'ts about dating during a divorce.

Strategic Reasons Not to Date During Divorce

Dating while divorcing may create serious resentment in your spouse, and he or she may make you pay during and after the divorce. In addition, your children may become upset seeing you with someone new when you aren't divorced. They may decide they don't want to visit you during or after the divorce. Alienating your spouse and children in the middle of a divorce is not a good plan. It's better to maintain a cordial relationship with your spouse and avoid unduly upsetting your children while the divorce is pending. A little thoughtfulness up front will pay big dividends when you co-parent with your ex-spouse and want a good relationship with your children after the divorce.

Legal Reasons Not to Date During Divorce

In Texas, you technically commit adultery if you have sexual relations with someone other than your spouse before your divorce is final. It's unlikely you will be formally charged with adultery, but having sexual relations with another person before your divorce is final can have negative financial consequences and could complicate custody arrangements. Adultery is one factor a Texas court may consider when awarding disproportionate assets to the innocent spouse. If you opted for a collaborative divorce, adultery may make it more difficult to agree about a parenting plan, and it could adversely affect your property division.

Emotional Reasons Not to Date During Divorce

Dating during your divorce may make you feel better about yourself and help you avoid experiencing the pain of separation. However, avoiding your pain and grief is not psychologically healthy. Sooner or later, you must experience those painful feelings of loss and learn to deal with them. Moreover, even though it may feel good to begin a new relationship while you are going through a divorce, you are probably not ready to handle the emotional issues associated with beginning a new relationship so soon. Everyone knows about the "rebound effect," which means relationships formed soon after a breakup rarely last. It will likely be months before you are emotionally ready for a new long-term relationship. You need time to heal and appreciate what went wrong in your marriage before you begin a new love. No matter how right this new person feels, you are almost certainly not in a good frame of mind to make the choice of a new mate.

Dos and Don'ts of Dating During Divorce

Don't even think about dating until you are out of the house and physically separated from your spouse. If you must date while your divorce is pending, it's better to socialize in a group. Don't introduce your new friend to the children until after the divorce is final, and don't have him or her sleep over with the children in the home. Most importantly, avoid a pregnancy while you're divorcing. Dealing with a pregnancy will complicate and prolong your divorce. Your spouse will be resentful, and you may have to wait until the baby is born to complete your divorce. Also, your children are likely to be upset if there is a pregnancy in the family while you are divorcing.

It's okay to socialize and network in a group during a divorce, but if you meet someone you like, be honest about your situation. Exchange contact information, but it's best to avoid one-on-one relationships until you are physically separated from your spouse. See a counselor or find a support group to help you cope with the pain, grief, and emotional stress of divorce, rather than masking it through dating. I understand you are miserable and lonely, but work through the pain; you will be glad you did later on.

Post-Divorce Estate Planning

How to Put Your Financial House in Order Following a Collaborative Divorce

In the middle of a divorce, the last thing on your mind is estate planning. However, once your divorce is final, you should put your financial house in order. Sections of the Texas Family and Estate Code will protect your assets from a former spouse. However, those statutes say nothing about who will inherit your estate. To make certain your assets pass to the proper loved ones, you should meet with an experienced estate planning attorney. A basic estate plan includes:

- Will or trust
- power of attorney
- Medical power of attorney
- Directive to physicians
- HIPAA document

A will determines how assets are distributed. A general power of attorney grants another person the power to act in your place if you are unable to handle your own affairs. A medical power of attorney gives another person authority to make health-care decisions when a physician certifies you are incompetent. A directive to physicians communicates your wishes about end-of-life care. Finally, a HIPAA release is an authorization to disclose protected health information to listed individuals.

The Texas Estate Code

The Estate Code revokes your former spouse's rights under a will or trust. However, the Estate Code only controls who will *not* inherit assets; it's no substitute for a new estate plan. Only a new plan can assure that your assets will be distributed according to your intent. Section 123.001 of the Estate Code says if you are divorced, all provisions of your predivorce will shall be read as if your former spouse and each relative of the former spouse did not survive you. Also, any provisions of the will that transferred property to an irrevocable trust shall be read as if your former spouse has given up his or her interest in the trust. Moreover, if a former spouse was named trustee of a trust, he or she will be treated as not having survived you.

The Texas legislature drafted chapter 123 of the Estate Code to protect your estate from your former spouse. However, it's neither easy nor safe for an executor to handle your estate based on a will drafted prior to divorce. The pre-divorce will must be read in conjunction with the Texas Estate Code and the Texas Family Code, which only determine what *can't* happen. This is needlessly complicated and potentially dangerous for your descendants because unexpected events can happen. Far better is to draft a post-divorce estate plan, clearly stating who shall take assets when you die and who will hold your power of attorney and medical power of attorney.

The Texas Estate Code also limits the rights of a former spouse to exercise a power of attorney or enjoy the benefits of an insurance policy or some retirement plans. However, qualified pension plans administered under federal law may not be covered by the Texas Estate Code. It's best to review these plans and file new beneficiary designations after the divorce is final. Section 751.053 of the Texas Estate Code says that unless a durable power of attorney is drafted specifically to survive divorce, the agency of a former spouse terminates when you are divorced. However, the Estate Code does not replace a former spouse with another agent. To do that, you need a post-divorce estate plan.

Texas Family Code

Section 9.301 of the Texas Family Code terminates the designation of a former spouse as beneficiary of a life insurance policy, unless the divorce decree specifically reappoints the former spouse as a beneficiary, you reappoint your former spouse as a beneficiary, or your former spouse is designated to receive the insurance proceeds as a trustee of your children. Texas Family Code §9.302 terminates the designation of your former spouse as a beneficiary of most individual retirement accounts, any employee stock option plan, savings plan, bonus, profit-sharing plan, or other benefit plan in force at the time the decree is final. However, if the divorce decree reappoints your former spouse as a beneficiary, you reappoint him or her as a beneficiary post-divorce, or he or she is designated to receive the proceeds of the employee benefit plan as a trustee for a child of the marriage, the reappointment stands. To be safe, it's a good idea to change the designation of beneficiaries on life insurance, pension plans, and bank or brokerage accounts after the divorce is final.

These statutory protections prevent your former spouse from taking assets if you die. However, many people don't name alternate beneficiaries in their will, insurance policies, pensions, or other employer compensation plans. Even if they do, the assets may pass to their minor children through the custody of an ex-spouse as a constructive trustee for the children. This is a situation ripe for misunderstanding at best and susceptible to fraud at worst. It's better to draft a new estate plan, to make certain your client's assets pass to loved ones without falling under the control of a former spouse.

www.ingramcontent.com/pod-product-compliance
Lightning Source LLC
Chambersburg PA
CBHW021952170526
45157CB00003B/950

* 9 7 8 1 4 8 0 8 5 3 7 9 9 *